AUGMENTED INTELLIGENCE

THE BUSINESS POWER OF HUMAN–MACHINE COLLABORATION

AUGMENTED INTELLIGENCE

THE BUSINESS POWER OF
HUMAN–MACHINE COLLABORATION

JUDITH HURWITZ
HENRY MORRIS
CANDACE SIDNER
DANIEL KIRSCH

CRC Press
Taylor & Francis Group
Boca Raton London New York

CRC Press is an imprint of the
Taylor & Francis Group, an **informa** business
AN AUERBACH BOOK

CRC Press
Taylor & Francis Group
6000 Broken Sound Parkway NW, Suite 300
Boca Raton, FL 33487-2742

First issued in paperback 2021

International Standard Book Number-13: 978-0-367-18489-6 (Hardback)
International Standard Book Number-13: 978-0-367-68787-8 (Paperback)

Visit the Taylor & Francis Web site at
http://www.taylorandfrancis.com

and the CRC Press Web site at
http://www.crcpress.com

Endorsements

"Our mission has always been to help clients apply AI to better predict and shape future outcomes, empower higher value work, and automate how work gets done. I have always said, 'AI will not replace managers, but managers who use AI will replace managers who don't.' This book delves into the real value that AI promises, to augment existing human intelligence, and in the process, dispels some of the myths around AI and its intended purpose."

— Rob Thomas
General Manager, IBM Data and AI

"This book enables managers, data analysts, business leaders, and AI experts to speak a common language, cutting through the jargon and hype to effectively harness augmented intelligence techniques for business decision-making. The authors provide a systematic framework for considering the uses and potential pitfalls of AI and machine learning in supporting business decision-making— always informed and shaped with up-to-date business practices in mind, for the real world where data resources are inherently dynamic and very fast changing."

— Stan Sclaroff
Dean of the College of Arts & Sciences, Boston University

"From my early days of commercializing IBM Watson, we realized that the real power of AI is not pitting humans against machines but pairing human and machine intelligence to unleash a new level of creativity and productivity at a scale we have never seen before. The authors of this book have done a wonderful job of articulating the real potential of AI—that of pairing human and machine intelligence to unleash a new level of creativity and productivity at a scale we have never seen before. I highly recommend reading this book to get a practical understanding of this complex and important subject."

— Manoj Saxena
Chairman, CognitiveScale and AI Global
First General Manager, IBM Watson
Founder and Serial Entrepreneur

"Given the current state of the market and the related discussion of deep learning and artificial intelligence, this book fills an immediate need. That need is of providing a realistic view of where intelligence-based systems will deliver the greatest value and utility to business and society. Judith, Henry, and I have been discussing analytical systems for decades, and the idea of augmented intelligence has been part of that dialog for as long as I can remember. Today, artificial intelligence is a charged topic, and the conversations range widely regarding the possible positive and negative outcomes. Augmented intelligence, the synergy of machine and human intelligence, is one of the most probable paths to creating sustainable, positive, and profitable outcomes through the blending of the unique traits of people and computing. If you want to understand how people and machines will come together and what they will deliver via augmented intelligence, you should read this book."

— John Thompson
Global Head, Advanced Analytics and Artificial Intelligence
CSL Behring

"I will have my entire management team read *Augmented Intelligence*. It's a refreshingly practical approach to the process and skill changes needed to take full advantage of advances in machine learning."

— David Kenny
CEO & Chief Diversity Officer, The Nielsen Company

"As an analytics and information communications technology professional, Augmented Intelligence resonates with me. I experience it daily through little things like automation getting me to an appointment on time. This book's exploration of this idea simultaneously reveals the benefits of augmentation and leaves the reader with afterthoughts on the ethical impacts of Augmented Intelligence and all aspects of AI. I would recommend this book to anyone wanting to rigorously explore the history and implication of Augmented and Machine Intelligence."

— Michael Hay
Senior Director of Product Management, Teradata
Founder, Cameron Solutions

"This book takes a didactic and in-depth approach to what Augmented Intelligence is and how to apply it. Augmented Intelligence is a way to use machine learning models and Artificial Intelligence tools to perform decision-making tasks. This approach to artificial intelligence complements and supports human intelligence, and is designed to optimize decision making. Augmented intelligence puts the human at the center of the decision-making process.

The book is a complete roadmap of Augmented Intelligence, covering from what Augmented Intelligence is, the entire data management cycle, the best way to build models, how to apply Augmented Intelligence to the new generation of business processes, to what is needed to build successful business cases. The book also addresses sensitive and critical issues in the adoption of Augmented Intelligence, such as the risks involved, as well as governance and ethics issues.

Certainly a highly recommended book that every professional interested in the future of technology should read."

— Marcus Borba
Data Science, Machine Learning, AI, Big Data,
Analytics and BI Global Influencer

"Augmented Intelligence provides a sober and critical analysis of current machine learning limitations and opportunities, and further shows the exceptional power of human–machine hybrid processes. This book provides an exceptional resource for understanding a crucial part of the machine learning field."

— Aaron Rasmussen
Founder & CEO, Outlier.Org
Co-founder, MasterClass, Inc.

"This team of world class experts has written an updated and comprehensive book covering augmented intelligence which clearly lays out how artificial intelligence has evolved as a practical and effective way to help businesses use advanced intelligence-based software techniques to help drive innovation, product development, better customer experience, and cost savings. If you are a business executive, information technology techie, or even an AI expert, you will want to not only read this, but also get copies for your business teams and colleagues."

— Eliot Weinman
Conference Founder and Chair, AI World

"Kudos to the authors for writing this book because Augmented Intelligence will become the future of work."

— Steve Ardire
AI Startup "Force Multiplier"
Active Speaker on Augmented Intelligence for the Future of Work

"In a world full of AI hype, fear, and loathing, *Augmented Intelligence* brings the reader a practical, commonsense view of how AI will not supplant humans, but work together with humans to improve business and government performance.

Simply put, humans need AI, and AI needs humans, in order to produce optimal outcomes. This book makes the case for augmented intelligence, discloses the risks involved with it, directs you on how to start leveraging augmented intelligence, and provides a glimpse into its future."

— Dave Kellogg
Serial Technology Executive and Author of Kellblog

Dedications

Judith Hurwitz

To my incredible family: my life partner and husband, Warren; my children,
Sara and David; and my beautiful grandsons, Jack and Sam.

Henry Morris

To my wonderful wife and life partner, Madelyn,
who always spurs me on to do my best work.

Candy Sidner

To Chuck Rich, my partner in all things AI and everything else.
I miss our conversations about what matters.

Daniel Kirsch

To my wife, Sara, and my sons, Jack and Sam, who will grow up in a
world that is greatly impacted by augmented intelligence.

Contents

Foreword

Artificial intelligence (AI) has been around for decades. AI has long piqued our imagination about what is possible with this powerful technology—for good and for evil. There are a vast number of instances in which AI has played a role in both our culture and in our desire to create more sophisticated systems. In fact, AI has captured the imagination of data scientists and fiction writers for decades. Alan Turing introduced seminal work on the meaning of artificial intelligence in the 1940s with his famous Turing test. In the 1960s project, ELIZA gave us a glimpse into the future of artificial intelligence–based communications. ELIZA, a project designed at MIT's artificial intelligence lab, was one of the first natural language processing computer programs that created a way for humans to communicate with machines. Early science fiction novels were obsessed with artificial intelligence. For example, science fiction novels such as *Metropolis*, written by 1925 by German writer Thea von Harbou, imagined the world in the year 2026, where humans and robots would live together but engage in massive conflicts.

In the last few years, AI has re-emerged due to two main factors: the unprecedented compute ability to crunch huge amounts of data with improved machine learning algorithms, and the brilliant marketing buzz of AI and ML.

However, artificial intelligence is way more than a passing fad. It is already a major part of our daily lives and will continue to accelerate. It is clear that there is an enormous amount of accessible data. We now have the ability to synthesize this massive amount of data in order to better understand everything from changing customer behaviors to the ability to anticipate what customers will want to buy in the future. With the movement toward AI, we can improve our ability to more accurately predict future business trends and requirements. AI's impact on modern medicine, for example, cannot be overlooked. AI will help to analyze complex data to support the physician's ability to customize effective treatments for patients. Across industries we are seeing important uses of AI that will be transformative.

Although AI has many types and forms, the most impactful in the immediate future is augmented intelligence. Augmented intelligence has profound ramifications because it empowers humans to truly leverage data to make better-informed decisions. The goal of augmented intelligence is not to replace people or automate them out of existence but to enable them to make better decisions based on complex data. In fact, the collaboration between humans and machines is the key enabler to our ability across industries to transition to the next stage of the information revolution.

One of the greatest impacts of augmented intelligence is the need to determine the accuracy of data in context. Understanding the context of data and the ability to actually trust this information is one of the most critical issues plaguing businesses today. If data can't be trusted or is inaccurate, decisions that are made based on that data could prove to be catastrophic. In addition to assuring data accuracy, data must be managed from a security, privacy, compliance, and risk perspective.

The book you are about to read is of great importance because we increasingly rely on machine learning and AI. Therefore, it is critical that we understand the ability to create an environment in which businesses can have the tools to understand data from a holistic perspective. What is imperative is to be able to make better decisions based on an understanding of the behavior and thinking of our customers so that we can take the best next action. This book provides a clear understanding of the impact of augmented intelligence on both society and business.

— Tsvi Gal, Managing Director
Enterprise Technology and Services
Morgan Stanley

Preface

Why This Book? Why Now?

Writing this book was a collaborative process among four seasoned professionals who have a common belief that when paired with human intuition and knowledge, artificial intelligence (AI) can change the world. The most pragmatic and useful way to benefit from AI and machine learning is to implement these powerful technologies as an augmentation to human intelligence. This hybrid approach—a partnership between humans and machines—is what is called *augmented intelligence*.

All four authors have a deep appreciation of the nuances of how we can harness the power of AI as a tool for transforming business. The value of our collaboration is that each of us brought a different perspective to a common goal of providing guidance and direction. Judith Hurwitz served as the author team leader. Judith has been a trusted advisor to many companies in a broad range of emerging technologies, ranging from data and analytics to cloud computing and business process. She has served on a variety of boards of advisors. In addition, Judith has coauthored 10 books, hundreds of e-books and articles, and is a frequent speaker and guest lecturer. Henry Morris is a technology thought leader with a PhD in philosophy from the University of Pennsylvania. Henry founded the analytics practice at the global research firm International Data Corporation (IDC), where he coined the industry term "analytic applications." Henry has decades of expertise in analytics applications, business process management software, and the complete data life cycle. Henry has consulted with a variety of organizations and businesses across the globe. Candy Sidner is a renowned AI research scientist with a PhD in artificial intelligence from MIT. She has written more than 100 research papers and is a fellow of the Association for the Advancement of Artificial Intelligence. Candy's involvement in the AI community stretches from some of the earliest days of AI to today's emerging research areas. Daniel Kirsch is an attorney, senior consultant, thought leader, and author. Dan has written dozens of e-books and white papers on topics focused on the cloud, data, security, and compliance. Dan's research focuses on emerging technologies and their impact on businesses as well as the security, governance, and compliance implications of new technology.

The best part of writing this book was our weekly team meetings, where we discussed and debated the meaning of the movement to augmented intelligence and the need to create a hybrid approach that pairs humans with machines. Therefore, we bring a unique perspective to both the business and technical nuances required to use artificial intelligence on a collaborative platform that makes human responses to complex problems more achievable.

There is no doubt that artificial intelligence is powerful and provides huge benefits in being able to determine patterns that impact business outcomes. At the same time, the context and nuances of any field are vast. To make well-informed decisions, you must be able to assess data while utilizing human intuition and an overall understanding of the field in question. The human brain can make certain judgments and decisions incredibly quickly and accurately, but these choices are nearly impossible to codify into an artificial intelligence system. For example, you can't rely on a programmatic bot to suggest the right mix of painkillers to a patient without having a full understanding of that patient's physical and emotional state. You also need to understand the community the patient lives in and what support services are available. A person may appear on paper to be stable but might have some underlying issues in their home life that will impact treatment options. There is no machine learning model that can capture the full context of a person and their environment without human assistance.

As a team, we felt it was our obligation to put the extraordinary hype about artificial intelligence and machine learning in perspective. Venture capitalists have poured billions of dollars into companies that are promising to transform entire markets with intelligent systems that will understand everything and automate almost any task one can imagine. In addition, there is a wide variety of companies focused on AI, ranging from newly formed ventures to some of the most well-established public companies that are planning for their future. There are futurists who will tell you that artificial intelligence–based systems will be able to think at the same level as humans. We believe this claim is a misconception. There is no one technology that will have the power and intuition of human experts. The ability to translate complex data into applied knowledge may hold the key to solving some of the most complex problems we as humans face. It is our view that it is not enough to have a machine learning model and all of the bells and whistles of new algorithms and new approaches to AI. What really matters is the context in which data is used to make decisions and to recognize that data is dynamically changing in concert with changing business processes. These observations about the changing context, types, and use of data call for AI to be used in collaboration with business experts.

Why You Should Read This Book

One of our goals for this book is to put artificial intelligence and machine learning in context so that professionals are armed with the tools they need to make faster and better decisions. There is so much excitement around the benefits and value of artificial intelligence that leads to misconceptions and poor practices. To be successful with machine learning requires a comprehensive understanding of data in context with the business problem you are addressing. It is mandatory to understand that machine learning models are dynamic and must evolve to reflect changes to data. At the same time, businesses have to understand the implications of relying on machine learning models to conduct business. Issues such as risks, ethics, and compliance are foundational issues that must be addressed or chaos and loss of reputation and business integrity can have dire consequences.

This book is aimed at three audiences: business leaders, technology managers, and AI experts who all need to have a common vocabulary and understand the importance of using AI and machine learning in a pragmatic way to solve real business problems. If you are a business leader, you need to understand the value of augmented intelligence in being able to differentiate your business from emerging competitors. If you are a technologist, you need to understand the power of AI and machine learning in context with the problems and needs of business professionals in your organization.

Within this book we provide business leaders with an understanding of the type of teams they need to create and the type of leadership management needs to provide. Technologists must have a detailed understanding of how to work with business leaders to create a platform for growth and differentiation. AI experts often focus on the technical nuances of their field without taking into account the requirement for designing new business processes and creating a platform that embraces changing data sources. If you are an expert in AI and machine learning, you need to understand the importance of the explainability of models in business environments. Although you may use sophisticated machine learning algorithms, you may not be able to have a clear understanding of how and why the system takes specific actions.

What Is in This Book

We divided this book into 10 chapters that focus on both the technical and business aspects of augmented intelligence.

Chapter 1: What Is Augmented Intelligence?

In this chapter, we define augmented intelligence as a way to use machine learning models and AI tools to perform decision-making tasks. Unlike traditional bots or automated processes, augmented intelligence is focused on humans collaborating with machines to discover results that are instrumental in aiding experts in making better informed decisions.

Chapter 2: The Technology Infrastructure to Support Augmented Intelligence

In this chapter we explain the innovations in infrastructure, including cloud computing and advances in machine learning models. This chapter explains the role of cloud computing in enabling businesses to have the capacity and performance to support complex data management. The chapter puts machine learning techniques into perspective as they relate to providing the foundation for the management of data that is accurate.

Chapter 3: The Cycle of Data

In this chapter, we explore the need for a consistent and predictable way to manage data sources, from data acquisition to data preparation, and the ability to build dynamic data models. It is important not to think of preparing and managing data as a one-step process. Rather, data has to be thought of as a continuum, since data sources are updated and changing constantly.

Chapter 4: Building Models to Support Augmented Intelligence

In this chapter, we explain what is required to build models intended for augmenting intelligence to support experts. It is clear that you have to select the most appropriate algorithms and then apply the necessary amount and type of data against the model. Testing and retesting as you add more data sources is a requirement for success.

Chapter 5: Augmented Intelligence in a Business Process

This chapter focuses on the great potential to apply augmented intelligence to the new generation of business processes. Humans and machines working in collaboration can have a powerful impact on the effectiveness of how organizations operate and manage customer relationships. Augmented intelligence overcomes the limitations of isolating human understanding from the massive amounts of both structured and unstructured data available to analyze complexity in record time. So, how does augmented intelligence change the way tasks are executed and the way that work is getting done?

Chapter 6: Risks in Augmented Intelligence

This chapter explains the potential business and technical risks when organizations take advantage of the power of AI and machine learning. The greatest risk for organizations leveraging machine learning models is to ensure that the correct data sources and the right amount of data is being used to solve a problem. If data scientists work in isolation from subject matter experts, the models may not reflect the real world. There is a huge risk that data will be misunderstood, leading to poor results.

Chapter 7: The Criticality of Governance and Ethics in Augmented Intelligence

This chapter focuses on the need to provide oversight of your augmented intelligence projects. Business teams are eager to leverage data to support revenue growth; they are often unaware of the potential legal, regulatory, and ethical implications of their project plan. At the same time, data scientists are often focused on gathering data, building models, and improving model accuracy. Issues such as governance and ethics often take a back seat. However, businesses have an obligation to follow prescribed governance rules. Likewise, organizations must make sure that they are handling data in a way that protects individuals' personal data.

Chapter 8: The Business Case for Augmented Intelligence

In this chapter, we focus on the need to build a business case for organizations to implement augmented intelligence. The value of this approach requires that technology leaders provide the business with an understanding of the value of both AI and machine learning techniques that can help subject matter experts make better decisions and outpace the competition.

Chapter 9: Getting Started on Your Journey to Augmented Intelligence

In this chapter, we explore the requirement to plan for implementing augmented intelligence. How you approach creating a strategy for augmented intelligence is complex. Therefore, business teams must start with a well-defined plan based on their business goals. To be successful, you need to have a project that is big enough that it can demonstrate to senior management that it can solve a real business need. At the same time, your project can't be so expansive that it will take too long and cost too much money to achieve a meaningful result.

Chapter 10: Predicting the Future of Augmented Intelligence

This chapter focuses on what we can expect in the future from augmented intelligence. We explore the ways that artificial intelligence and machine learning models will change the way we work. The chapter looks into the future of the value in codifying knowledge so that experts can do a better job by leveraging and codifying the massive amounts of information inside business data sources.

About the Authors

Judith S. Hurwitz

Judith is a technology consultant and strategist, analyst, author, and thought leader. As president of a research and consulting firm—Hurwitz & Associates—Judith's work has focused on emerging technology, including cloud computing, big data, software development, computing management, and security. Prior to starting Hurwitz & Associates, Judith founded two other companies—CycleBridge, a life science software consulting firm, and Hurwitz Group, Inc., a research and analyst firm. She has worked at various corporations, including Apollo Computer and John Hancock. Judith serves on several advisory boards for emerging companies, and she is a frequent speaker at technology conferences as well as a guest lecturer.

In 2011, she authored a business leadership book, *Smart or Lucky? How Technology Leaders Turn Chance into Success* (Jossey-Bass, 2011). Judith is a co-author of nine books in addition to *Augmented Intelligence*, including *Cognitive Computing and Big Data Analytics* (Wiley Publishing, 2015), *Cloud for Dummies* (Wiley Publishing, 2020), and *Big Data for Dummies* (Wiley Publishing, 2013). In addition, she contributed a chapter to *Intuition, Trust, and Analytics* (CRC Press/Taylor & Francis Group, 2018). Judith holds B.S. and M.S. degrees from Boston University. She is a member of Boston University's College of Arts & Sciences Dean's Advisory Board.

Henry Morris

Henry is a consultant and thought leader in applying analytics, business processes, and governance to business systems. He served as Senior Vice President for Worldwide Software and Services Research and was a Research Fellow at International Data Corporation (IDC). During his tenure at IDC, Henry founded the research practice on analytics, coining the now industry-standard term "analytic applications." Henry is renowned for his work on analytics software that is purpose-built to support decision-oriented business processes. He has provided consulting advice on applied analytics to some of the most prominent vendors and corporations.

Prior to his work at IDC, Henry was a senior marketing manager for database and applications development and a technical writer at Digital Equipment Corporation. He was the author of *Introduction to Database Development,* which described detailed strategies for balancing transactional and analytical database access. Henry was also Assistant Professor of Philosophy and Religion at Colgate University, Lecturer at Tufts University Experimental College (artificial intelligence and the changing workplace), and Lecturer at Northeastern University and Bentley University (in technical writing). He has a B.A. with distinction from the University of Michigan and a Ph.D. in philosophy from the University of Pennsylvania.

Candace Sidner

Candace (Candy) is a computer scientist, researcher, and consultant with a long-standing interest in human communication and collaboration, and their application to agents, robots, and interfaces. Candy is especially focused on those systems that are using gesture, social behavior, speech, and natural language. She is a Research Professor at Worcester Polytechnic Institute (WPI). She was Principle Investigator (PI) of the Always On Relational Agent project with Chuck Rich at WPI and Tim Bickmore at Northeastern University, and co-PI for the ONR-sponsored WPI project: Collaborative Robot Learning from Demonstration Using Hierarchical Task Networks. Candy has recently worked on multimodal (including gesture) interfaces using a humanoid robot for the role of engagement in conversation, and on interfaces, including those with speech, involving collaborative interface agents using DISCO. Candy has also been a research scientist at a number of companies, including Mitsubishi Electronic Research Labs, and served as a Division Scientist at BAE Systems.

Candy is a Fellow and past Councilor of the Association for the Advancement of Artificial Intelligence, was elected a Fellow of the Association for Computational Linguistics, and is a senior member of the IEEE. She serves on the editorial board of the Springer *Journal of Multimodal User Interfaces.* She has been an associate editor of the journal *ACM Transactions on Intelligent Interactive Systems,* an associate editor of the journal *Artificial Intelligence* (2008–2012), and was president of the Association for Computational Linguistics (1989).

Candy received her B.S. in Mathematics from Kalamazoo College, an M.S. degree in Computer Science from the University of Pittsburgh, and a Ph.D. from MIT in Computer Science.

Daniel Kirsch

Daniel (Dan) is a consultant, analyst, and thought leader focused on how emerging technologies such as AI, machine learning, and advanced analytics are impacting businesses. Dan is particularly interested in how businesses use these emerging technologies to alter their approaches to information security, governance, risk, and ethics. Dan provides advisory services directly to leadership at technology vendors that design and deliver security solutions to the market. He assists them in aligning their solutions with enterprise requirements. Dan is viewed as an expert in understanding security solutions and mapping them to the complex needs of business across industries. He developed the Hurwitz & Associates security audit and assessment tools. These tools help customers determine how well they are achieving compliance, and outline practical next steps.

Dan earned his B.A. in Political Science from Union College in New York and a J.D. from Boston College Law School, where he focused on emerging corporate strategies and intellectual property. As an attorney, Dan represented start-ups, cloud computing ventures, and young companies seeking financing. Dan is a co-author of *Cloud for Dummies* (John Wiley & Sons 2020), *Hybrid Cloud for Dummies* (John Wiley & Sons, 2012), as well as reports and custom publications in the areas of security, mobility, and analytics.

Chapter 1

What Is Augmented Intelligence?

Introduction

Will artificial intelligence (AI) take over all of our jobs and create a world where we no longer have to think for ourselves? Although this may seem preposterous, there are many scientists, professors, and futurists who believe that we as humans are replaceable by machines. Our view is that we have reached a turning point in how intelligent machines can automate well-defined tasks—even as the underlying data changes. But machine intelligence is also driving the transformation of business processes, changing how work gets done. Although it is true that some jobs will be lost as artificial intelligence is utilized by businesses, for many, artificial intelligence will help transform and augment their job functions and responsibilities. A new breed of hybrid business professional will be needed—a person who combines business knowledge with expertise in data and its use in building predictions that can drive intelligent decision making.

Being able to allow humans to create sophisticated data models has enabled us to reach newer levels of machine learning than ever before. However, that is only half of the story. In reality, humans are different from machines. A machine can accomplish well-defined goals, but a human has the ability to grasp the context of the data and knowledge across a broad spectrum of issues. A tiny observation or element of data can totally change the outcome. Simply put, a machine cannot ingest all of the data in all of the various contexts to keep up with what a smart human can do. Artificial intelligence, or more precisely, machine learning models, learn from the data they are given. These models continually get smarter and can help make better decisions based on where the data leads them.

Defining Augmented Intelligence

We maintain in this book that beyond artificial intelligence, there is augmented intelligence, which can significantly transform how we can leverage knowledge, artificial intelligence (especially machine learning), and various tools that support advanced analytics. So, what is augmented intelligence? Augmented intelligence is an approach that uses tools from artificial intelligence to perform well-defined tasks, such as those that are part of decision making. But for augmented intelligence, the human works in collaboration with machines. Humans need to evaluate the results of the automated tasks, make decisions in non-routine situations, and also assess if and when the data must be changed due to changing business needs and demands.

Though a more routine decision can be automated for autonomous machine operation, the more ambiguous or riskier tasks are left to human partners. For example, insurance companies are making big investments in artificial intelligence to automate underwriting decisions. Fully autonomous decisions via machine intelligence tend to be used for smaller policies, wherein the risk is more limited. For larger, more complex policies, machine recommendations provide assistance to human underwriters who still have the decision-making authority.[1]

Weak versus Strong Augmentation

There are a variety of ways that augmentation and AI techniques can be used to help with business tasks. Therefore, there is a spectrum from weak augmentation to strong augmentation. When we say weak, it doesn't mean that it is poor; it just means that it is intended to automate a task performed by a human worker. It simply eliminates the task done by the human in favor of doing that same task by a combination of AI techniques such as machine learning, natural language processing, and data analytics. Weak augmentation can enhance a business by making the tasks more efficient and cost effective. However, the actual cost savings must be calculated to reflect the use of personnel to periodically gather new data as well as to review and test the AI tools that replace human workers.

Strong augmentation uses AI techniques but combines them with human assessments to change business processes. The new process is a revised workflow that takes advantage of tasks that only machines can perform or that machines perform best with tasks that only human workers can perform or that humans excel at.

The Goal of Human–Machine Collaboration

The goal of augmented intelligence is to enable human–machine collaboration to produce positive outcomes that neither machines nor humans alone can achieve. The steps needed to implement augmented intelligence are as follows:

- Decide whether to change the business process and task flow for human–machine cooperation to drive better outcomes
- Select which tasks and decisions within the business process to automate
- Determine the proper AI tools
- Determine what data to acquire to better understand and model the business and customers
- Build the data models
- Test the results for reliability and accuracy

Learning requires that we feed a model with the right amount of data at the right velocity to continue to learn as things change. Why? Because a system is only as good as the data it contains. For situations where you can frame and define the problem, machine learning models are an incredibly powerful way to solve problems.

Subject matter experts, for example, can use machine learning models to capture and interpret massive amounts of data in a way that the human brain cannot absorb or remember. The secret for companies to gain true competitive advantage is the ability to gain understanding of the knowledge and data that these businesses already possess or that they need to acquire. Therefore, those professionals with deep context and understanding of their industries are in an incredibly powerful position to be successful. These are the hybrids—combining business knowledge with the ability to leverage machine-generated predictions derived from relevant business data.

Augmented intelligence systems are designed to work with people and thereby extend human intelligence. Below are two examples that illustrate the possibilities of combining human and machine intelligence to achieve better outcomes than either machines or humans alone. The first is humans and machines joining forces to play a competitive version of chess, and the second is a case of retail store employees working with automated video analysis. In both cases we are combining machine and human intelligence to do work in a different way to yield better results.

How Augmented Intelligence Works in the Real World

Complex games such as chess are one of the areas that have been used to demonstrate the potential power of artificial intelligence. In 1997, an IBM supercomputer called Deep Blue was able to defeat Garry Kasparov, the reigning world chess champion.[2] It was a stunning achievement and suggested that an intelligent system could truly think. But could collaboration between a machine and humans do even better? Freestyle chess is a form of advanced chess based on the ability of humans to collaborate with machine-based contestants. In the 2014 competition, the winning Team Anson Williams consisted of three people with a passion for chess (but not master players) and a machine learning–based chess program with access to a massive database of millions of chess games. The machine recommended the most promising moves at each decision point during the match. But it was the responsibility of the team leader to make the move, after considering the machine's recommendation and being careful not to take too much of the limited clock time. The results have been very successful, enabling the team to defeat other hybrid man–machine teams, machine-only teams, and even several grandmasters.[3]

Freestyle chess demonstrates the power of blending human and machine intelligence—augmented intelligence. The key, noted by former world chess champion Garry Kasparov, is to provide an interface that enables effective man–machine interaction and collaboration.[4] These hybrid man–machine systems address the limitations of either human or machine intelligence acting alone to yield the best outcomes.

Can this human–machine collaboration work in the business world? The answer is yes. Take the example of retail stores that have to deal with the costly problem of inventory loss or "shrinkage" on a regular basis. There are many reasons why retailers suffer losses, including theft, fraud, or human error. One software company based in Cork, Ireland—Everseen Ltd.—created software for retailers intended to address this loss problem. The software uses video analytics powered by machine learning to rapidly analyze video images from cameras in the store. The software can analyze the videos much faster and more accurately than security personnel. Machines, unlike humans, can analyze massive amounts of video feeds at a time. If an exception to the normal checkout process is detected, the machine intelligence program can alert a store employee who can take corrective action before the goods leave the store. In effect, the surveillance process has been changed to incorporate coordinated machine and human intelligent activities. Reducing these losses can provide a significant saving to retailers.

Improving Traditional Applications with Machine Intelligence

The combination of machine intelligence (analyzing the video feeds) and store personnel (handling the exceptions) is an improvement over the traditional point-of-sale processes that relied on human surveillance alone and that failed to detect most of the suspicious events. As in the freestyle chess example, a combination of machine and human actions—"augmented intelligence"—achieved better results than humans acting alone.

From a technology perspective, current augmented intelligence systems and their underlying artificial intelligence tools require access to large sets of data. These intelligent systems are developed using technologies including machine learning, natural language processing, and predictive analytics.

Machine learning uses a variety of algorithms that iteratively learn from data to improve, describe data, and predict outcomes. The resulting models improve their performance based on exposure to new data, rather than by explicit programming.

Natural Language Processing (NLP) is the ability of computer systems to process text written or recorded in a language used for human communication (such as English or French). Human "natural language" is filled with ambiguities. For example, one word can have multiple meanings, depending on how it is used in a sentence. In addition, the meaning of a sentence can change dramatically just by adding or removing a single word. NLP enables computer systems to interpret the meaning of language and to generate natural language responses.

Predictive analytics is a statistical approach consisting of algorithms and techniques that can be used on both structured and unstructured data to determine future outcomes.

Technological advances in storage, processing, and analytics have made it economically feasible to deliver machine-intelligent predictions on a scale not possible before. These predictions can augment human intelligence by identifying the course of action that is most likely to produce the best outcome.

Intelligent predictions depend on a rich store of relevant data. Without good quality data, there cannot be good quality predictions. Therefore, the evaluation of where to apply augmented intelligence must begin with assessing the availability and quality of relevant data. The relevant data has to be ingested, prepared, and validated through testing and training.

Historical Perspective

In the late 1950s, artificial intelligence was conceived as a way to enable computers to automate routine tasks without human intervention. Could a computer use mathematics to translate the working of neurons in the brain into a set of logical constructs and models that would mimic the workings of the human mind?

John McCarthy (then at MIT and later at Stanford) convened a workshop at Dartmouth College in the summer of 1956 on the subject of what he called "artificial intelligence." He advanced the following idea for the conference:

Every aspect of learning or any other feature of intelligence can be so precisely described that a machine can be made to simulate it.[5]

Herbert Simon, an artificial intelligence pioneer and one of the attendees, wrote, "[M]achines will be capable, within twenty years, of doing any work a man can do."[6] Marvin Minsky, another artificial intelligence pioneer and attendee, claimed, "[W]ithin a generation . . . the problem of creating 'artificial intelligence' will be substantially solved."[7] These researchers believed that artificial intelligence could enable machines to replace humans in all types of work, especially those requiring cognition.

Just a few years after the Dartmouth AI workshop, another group of computer scientists began to anticipate that computers could be used as a tool for collaboration with humans. Two visionary researchers who took this position were J. C. R. Licklider and Douglas Engelbart—pioneers in human/machine interaction.

Today's augmented intelligence incorporates both the heritage of artificial intelligence (for building intelligent system) and the heritage of human–computer interactivity pioneered by Licklider and Engelbart (for enabling human–machine collaboration to get work done).

J. C. R. Licklider was a psychologist and computer scientist who foresaw modern styles of human–computer interaction based on networks of computers and applications designed to enable human–machine collaboration. His 1960 paper, "Man–Computer Symbiosis," provided a vision for augmented intelligence in which men and computers work together to make decisions and control a "complex situation."[7] Licklider carefully outlined the distinct roles of humans and computers in such a situation:

Man–computer symbiosis is an expected development in cooperative interaction between men and electronic computers. It will involve very close coupling between the human and the electronic members of the partnership. The main aims are 1) to let computers facilitate formulative thinking as they now facilitate the solution of formulated problems, and 2) to enable men and computers to cooperate in making decisions and controlling complex situations without inflexible dependence on predetermined programs. In the anticipated symbiotic partnership, men will set the goals, formulate the hypotheses, determine the criteria, and perform the evaluations. Computing machines will do the routinizable work that must be done to prepare the way for insights and decisions in technical and scientific thinking. Preliminary analyses indicate that the symbiotic partnership will perform intellectual operations much more effectively than man alone can perform them.

Rather than envisioning a future in which a machine would replace people, Licklider predicted a beneficial division of labor between machines and people. Machines would perform the more "routine tasks, giving people time to think and the opportunity to develop more sophisticated computer programs that they could interact with. The combination or what Licklider called the "symbiotic partnership" of human and machine would perform intelligent operations better than individual workers alone.[8]

Douglas Engelbart wanted to make computers better for people to use as a way to expand human intelligence. He anticipated leveraging advances in artificial intelligence to achieve his goals. Although Engelbart did not envision what we now think of as augmented intelligence, his ideas were an important ingredient in the idea of human–machine collaboration. To advance these ideas, Engelbart established the Augmentation Research Center at the Stanford Research Institute (SRI), where innovations in user interface styles, such as the first computer mouse, were developed. In his 1962 paper, "Augmenting Human Intellect: A Conceptual Framework,"[9] he explained that the goal of augmented intelligence is to increase the capacity of humans to solve problems:

> By "augmenting human intellect" we mean increasing the capability of a man to approach a complex problem situation, to gain comprehension to suit his particular needs, and to derive solutions to problems. Increased capability in this respect is taken to mean a mixture of the following: more-rapid comprehension, better comprehension, the possibility of gaining a useful degree of comprehension in a situation that previously was too complex, speedier solutions, better solutions, and the possibility of finding solutions to problems that before seemed insoluble. . . . We refer to a way of life in an integrated domain where hunches, cut-and-try, intangibles, and the human "feel for a situation" usefully co-exist with powerful concepts, streamlined terminology and notation, sophisticated methods, and high-powered electronic aids.

Engelbart's idea of "augmentation" gave the name "augmented intelligence" to the "symbiotic relationship" between man and machine previously described by Licklider. Both Licklider and Engelbart searched for new ways to achieve better outcomes through human–machine collaboration, rather than the machine-only vision of the early artificial intelligence researchers. The related ideas of Licklider and Englebart provide the foundation for today's work in augmented intelligence, where machines augment human performance. Neither of these groups of researchers could have imagined the evolution of the original concepts of artificial intelligence and human–computer interfaces that have led to today's implementations of augmented intelligence.

The Three Principles of Augmented Intelligence

When is augmented intelligence superior to either human intelligence or machine intelligence alone? We assert the following three principles on why machines alone are not the future for business success:

1. There are limits to how well humans can understand the content and scope of their data. There are limits to how much data an individual can absorb and understand. For example, these limitations are evident when analyzing large data sets, streaming data, and complex unstructured data. Machine intelligence can supplement these capabilities to help people understand data.
2. Humans must also make the decision regarding where and when to deploy automation and machine learning. There are a variety of considerations that need to be understood. First, when does it make economic sense to apply machine learning techniques? Second, does the organization have the right data and the right infrastructure to support a major change? Third, decision makers need to understand the strategic intent of the platform. Complex decision making will require humans to collaborate with machine intelligence. In all situations, humans are responsible for providing governance and controls to address machine intelligence limitations, such as algorithmic bias.
3. Combining human and machine intelligence in a redesigned business process can overcome the limitations of humans or machines acting alone to produce the best outcomes. Humans are the ones that need to use their knowledge to redesign business processes because the technology is not going to make the difficult decisions to transform the business.

Explaining the Principles of Augmented Intelligence

Implementing an augmented intelligence strategy must incorporate a combination of efforts. One of the benefits of augmented intelligence is that it becomes a tool to assist humans in gaining better insights and understanding of complex data. Humans simply cannot sift through mounds of complex data alone. In most fields, there is simply too much data—both historic and current—to be able to make sense of the underlying nuances. At the same time, the power of AI has to be harnessed and governed. Is the data accurate? Does it include private information that must be secured from view? Who is allowed to see the data? Is the data being distributed for other purposes so that controls are lost? All of these issues must be established to manage the power of AI. Finally, one of the greatest potentials of augmented intelligence is the ability to redesign a business process based on the data that is ingested. Changing a process can be a complex task based on rethinking how business is accomplished today and how it will change in the future.

Machine Intelligence Addresses Human Intelligence Limitations

Human intelligence has limitations that can cause us to make suboptimal decisions. We are constrained in the range of experiences and information that we can rely on when making decisions. We also have limitations on our ability to properly understand the hidden biases that led to decision-making risks. With the support of machine intelligence, individuals can be advised about problems that can impact the quality of a decision. Machine intelligence assistance can lead to better-informed decisions.

To consider how augmented intelligence addresses known limitations in human decision making, let's start with a now-famous example.

There was not one single factor that led to the Great Recession of 2008. Many financial observers have pointed to a series of bad decisions by many actors within the financial and real estate industries. These decisions included the following:

- Subprime lenders approved home mortgages for buyers who were not credit worthy and thus likely to default.
- Investment banks bundled bad mortgages into new instruments (mortgage-backed securities).
- Insurance companies issued new investment vehicles that attempted to protect issuers and investors from the risks inherent in mortgage-backed securities (credit default swaps).
- Credit rating bureaus issued high ratings to the mortgage-backed securities and credit default swaps.
- Buyers relied on these credit ratings when making investment decisions.

Each of these factors alone would not necessarily have led to a major market collapse. However, the combined effect of all of these events was dramatic. If regulators or financial analysts had been able to understand the context of these decisions they might have been able to take corrective action to avoid unsustainable risks to the financial system.

In the years leading up to the Great Recession, young bank managers approved mortgages for buyers with insufficient credit. They were assuming that the value of the property would be adequate protection in case of default. In the experience of these young managers, real estate values always went up—they never went down. With their limited experience, they were unable to assess correctly the probability that real estate prices would decline or remain steady rather than continue to increase. Unaware of the history of real estate price fluctuations, these managers could not properly assess the risk involved in approving a loan to an individual with low credit standing. Believing that prices would never decrease, they wrongfully assumed that the property would provide adequate security for the loan.

This example illustrates a common limitation to human decision making—lack of access to critical relevant information and inherent biases. Machine intelligence can address this limitation if given the proper data. Unlike the young bank managers, machines can take account of large data sets of real estate transactions and borrower histories over many years to identify patterns and accurately predict the probability of default. Unlike the young bank managers, if machines had had access to historical real estate transaction data, they would have learned that real estate prices do not always rise.

Another limitation on human decision making is psychological. Behavioral economists, inspired by the work of Amos Tversky and Daniel Kahneman, have shown that humans have psychological limitations that impact their decision making, particularly under conditions of risk and uncertainty. Their writings in the 1970s and 1980s explained the cognitive basis for human errors that resulted from poor judgment and biases[10–12] and developed prospect theory.[13] Two examples are loss aversion and confirmation bias.

- *Loss aversion* is the act of avoiding a loss even when the probability of the negative output is very low. For example, keeping your savings in a savings account with little interest is low risk. However, inflation will reduce your future purchasing power. Had you invested in an index fund, risk would likely be tolerable, and your savings would have been dramatically improved.
- *Confirmation bias* occurs when an individual seeks out information that agrees with our assumptions. For example, it is possible to find literature and past examples wherein putting money in a savings account would have been a better decision than investing in a diversified fund. However, the majority of research and literature would contradict this assertion.

We also rely on heuristics or rules of thumb that enable us to make quick decisions—but these shortcuts may be contradicted by predictions developed by a careful analysis of the relevant data. These limitations challenge the prevailing view of economists since Adam Smith (from the 1700s) that humans always select the alternative with the highest expected outcome.

The value of augmented intelligence is that it can help individuals overcome human limitations. Machines can provide guidance to a human decision maker based on an analysis of large volumes of relevant data. By observing patterns in the data set, machine intelligence can build predictions and then recommend the course of action with the highest expected return. In some cases, machines can even identify a new course of action not considered by the human decision maker, such as a diagnosis of a rare condition not previously considered by the physician.

Human Intelligence Should Provide Governance and Controls

The previous examples show how machine assistance can help us overcome human limitations. In parallel, machine intelligence has limitations that require human intervention. Humans decide where machine intelligence should be applied—to which domain and to which decisions. And humans have the responsibility to provide continued oversight, testing, and monitoring of the operations of the algorithms. The limited ability of machine intelligence to understand the full context for a decision can lead to unintended adverse consequences. This limitation needs to be addressed by human intelligence in the form of governance and controls.

Nicholas Bostrum, in his book *Superintelligence: Paths, Dangers, and Strategies*, provides sobering examples of the risk of unchecked, uncontrolled artificial intelligence.[14] Suppose a machine is given the task of maximizing the production of paper clips. In response to this request, the machine leverages all the earth's resources to the sole goal of producing paper clips. Likewise, an autonomous vehicle is given the command to take a passenger to the airport as fast as possible. Obeying this command, the vehicle is found smashing through roadblocks, hitting pedestrians, and so on in order to fulfill the request. This is reminiscent of children's stories where a maxim is taken too literally and causes unexpected adverse consequences. King Midas, from Greek mythology, relishes the prospect of increasing his wealth through his ability to turn ordinary objects into gold, not anticipating that he could turn people like his own children into lifeless gold statues.[15]

Another governance risk occurs when there is algorithmic bias. This condition arises when the data used to train a machine learning model reinforces a person's or organization's underlying assumptions (whether explicit or subconscious). Consider the following example: There are machine learning–based programs designed to help a company select the most qualified candidates for job openings. The company selects the data based on current company employees. The system learns from the data set (using a technique known as "supervised learning") about the attributes of employees who have been successful in the company, identifying which attributes are the best predictors of a successful employee. With this learning from the training data set, you ask the system to apply this prediction to new data coming in from the resumes received by the firm. Resumes of candidates who have attributes that were shown to predict success are then selected for interviews, whereas those who do not have these attributes are rejected.

Although this seems straightforward, there is an unforeseen problem. Suppose that traditionally the company has hired primarily white males. Since the model used only data from existing employees, the system will only select candidates that match historical data. Thus, the data set is biased, and the new algorithm inherits those biases. The company's hiring team will be frustrated by the candidates selected (no women or minorities will be selected), not understanding that the problem is in the data, not the process.

Human governance and controls are needed to guard against algorithmic bias in the machine intelligence resume-matching algorithm. The algorithm should be tested before going operational. Do the recommendations leave out populations of candidates based on known employment discrimination factors such as ethnicity, color, or gender? If such bias is detected, a new unbiased data set will be needed to fix the problem.

In the case of the recruiting algorithm, the data set would be expanded to include a broader population of candidate types. Retrain the algorithm on the expanded data set and test the new results for bias. If the initial results are promising in eliminating bias, continue to follow up with ongoing monitoring to see that the algorithm continues to perform in an unbiased manner. Machines do not have a life of their own. People have the responsibility to deploy machine intelligence safely and ethically.

Machine learning, natural language processing, and predictive analytics technologies need human perspective and judgment to be applied to specialized domains and problems. It is our responsibility to govern the technology, establishing where and how machine intelligence should be used, choosing the widest data sets possible, establishing controls for its operation, and continually monitoring the results.

Summary: How Augmented Intelligence and Artificial Intelligence Differ

Artificial intelligence and augmented intelligence systems are both built on technologies such as machine learning, natural language processing, and predictive analytics. But the goal of an artificial intelligence system is to simulate human cognitive capabilities in a system that can function independently of human agents. By contrast, the goal of an augmented intelligence system is to enhance human intelligence, enabling a human–machine collaboration to get work done.

- Machine intelligence addresses human limitations in decision making and problem solving. Machine intelligence yields predictions of future outcomes based on the analysis of large data sets. These predictions take into account hundreds of factors and determine which ones have the greatest impact on future outcomes. Machines deliver these predictions in the form of recommendations for improving decision making. Human decision makers do not have the ability to consider the vast amounts of data that a machine can analyze. Humans also can fall victim to adverse psychological factors such as risk avoidance or confirmation bias. With a machine assist, human decision making can be improved.
- Human governance is needed to address machine intelligence limitations. Machine intelligence requires human oversight. Humans are responsible for governing, monitoring, and auditing the process as a whole to ensure that it complies with corporate, legal, and ethical standards. Moreover, machines cannot perform all the work performed every day by men and women. It is the responsibility of humans to determine how and when machine intelligence should be used. Humans are also responsible for developing and executing the strategy for data acquisition, ensuring that there is a rich and varied set of relevant data for model development and deployment.

An augmented intelligence system builds predictions and identifies which course of action is likely to deliver the optimal result to human decision makers. Blending human intelligence and machine intelligence overcomes the limitations of each and leads to the best outcomes for many classes of problems. To achieve the best outcomes, it is not enough to automate specific tasks according to the task flow of the existing business process. The key for realizing benefits is to redesign the process continually to enable man-machine collaborative interaction. The boundaries between human and machine responsibilities continue to change with advances in machine intelligence.

Augmented intelligence blends human and machine intelligence in a redesigned business process to achieve better outcomes than either humans or machines could achieve alone. Throughout this book, we will provide examples of how augmented intelligence changes work processes across diverse businesses from finance to procurement to operations to marketing.

Chapter 2

The Technology Infrastructure to Support Augmented Intelligence

Introduction

The field of artificial intelligence (AI) has existed since the 1950s when visionaries imagined being able to turn computers into thinking machines that could mimic and even surpass the ability of humans to learn. Why did it take almost six decades for the dream of artificial intelligence and machine learning (ML) to emerge? There is a convergence of technologies that have come together to lead the market towards the reality of machine learning, artificial intelligence, and, finally, to augmented intelligence. In this chapter, we discuss the technology infrastructure that has emerged to support augmented intelligence.

Beginning with Data Infrastructure

What are the fundamental changes that have allowed artificial intelligence and machine learning to experience a rebirth? It begins with having the right infrastructure in place to manage data. How can an organization manage high volumes of complex data in order to build and maintain machine learning models? To be successful, it is mandatory to manage all of the required data in a systematic manner so that data being leveraged is well understood and accurate. Therefore, the journey to augmented intelligence begins with managing data. Simply put, you can't attempt to do true augmented intelligence until you have a lot of the right data. Big data in this context has to be approached in a methodical manner. Why is now the time right for the dramatic transition to the combination of machine learning and human intelligence? We are in the midst of an era of convergence in which advances in technology have accelerated our ability to manage and understand data. Later in this chapter, we provide an overview of the type of machine learning techniques that are being applied to this well-managed data. But first, we need to understand the underlying hardware systems and platforms needed to put the data to use for augmented intelligence.

What a Difference the Cloud Makes

Many advanced thinkers in the mid part of the 20th century anticipated that computing would become a utility. They imagined that like electricity, computing could become a simple utility that a business would plug into in order to unleash unlimited power at a fraction of the cost. The idea of Internet-driven services were common in academic circles through the use of the Advanced Research Projects Agency Network (ARPANET)—a government-funded project to help the military and academic researchers exchange information over a network.

True commercial cloud services emerged in 2002 when Amazon introduced Amazon Web Services (AWS), followed by the launch of Elastic Compute Cloud (EC2) four years later. Ironically, Amazon began selling its web services when it implemented more cloud services than it needed to operate its online commerce platform. It became clear that the ability to add compute and storage capability on demand was a game changer. The architectural model of the cloud services combined with a new pricing model was instrumental in the transition to commercial machine learning and artificial intelligence. It wasn't just that the price per CPU hour of computing was low and the price to store data was a fraction of previous financial models. The key issue was that the underlying architecture was designed to support unanticipated scaling and management of data.

A multitude of vendors understanding the potential revolution of the cloud began to build hardware enablement—newer powerful chips and graphic processing units (GPUs) turbocharged the performance of machine learning models that needed to use massive amounts of data to solve complex analytics for machine learning models. Techniques such as GPUs enabled near real-time processing of images, videos, and complex data.

The Cloud Changes Everything

The question then became, how much could you accomplish if there are virtually no limits on computing power or storage? The answer was simple: Without physical constraints, anything was possible. This transformation to cloud computing has opened the door to innovation that is changing both the maturation of data science and the ability of businesses to accelerate their growth. Combining the power and economics of cloud computing with the innovations in machine learning and artificial intelligence has created a revolution that will touch every industry, every business and business process, and every human activity. All human endeavors and processes will be impacted by this renaissance. The real question is, how can we harness this innovation to support the power of the human brain to make better-informed decisions that can change everything?

As we discussed in Chapter 1, artificial intelligence is the umbrella concept that incorporates methods, tools, languages, and algorithms. With cloud infrastructure, it is now possible to provide sophisticated tools that can transform what had only been possible through laborious manual efforts. The efficiency and pricing structure of the cloud has transformed the way data can be used to move to a new generation of AI. With this platform in place, it is not surprising that machine learning and artificial intelligence are experiencing a renaissance. So, with this power in place, how do we use cloud services to transform our ability to harness the power of data.

Big Data as Foundation

In the past, data analysts were locked into analyzing data at a superficial level: How many widgets did I sell last month? How much did they cost to make and how much profit did my business unit make? As businesses grew more complex with more lines of business, more business partners, and more innovation, it become more difficult to simply ask direct questions and gain the level of insight needed to be competitive. Business leaders wanted to understand the impact on the future. Would it be possible to use data to anticipate the future and determine new directions and new business models never seen before? Leaders wanted to understand hidden patterns in their vast stores of data and information about their products, services, and customers. They also wanted to begin to put their data to work in order to plan for the future. What will customers expect to purchase next year? In other words, how can a business anticipate the future?

As the industry changed with the advent of the cloud and new hardware architectures that were more agile and efficient, the ability to conduct advanced analytics grew at a rapid pace. With the technological advances, it was conceivable to rapidly collect and automatically process the data. Now, it was possible to provide more advanced analytics techniques such as data mining, data lakes, and predictive analytics, and to leverage machine learning algorithms. The promise of advanced analytics has been to use massive amounts of data to accelerate our ability to make sense of a chaotic world. The ultimate goal, as we have explained in Chapter 1, is to move from simply getting answers to questions to delve deeply into the context and meaning of complex data techniques based on codifying knowledge—augmented intelligence. But before we satisfy that goal, we have to understand the changing nature of data management technologies and architectures. Therefore, you have to approach big data in a methodical manner. Big data begins with understanding the data sources—what they mean and how they are related to each other. Once you establish the data sources, you need to understand the relationships between data elements and sources. The data needs to be clean and well understood in context. At the end, it is critical to find the context, anomalies, and patterns from all sorts of data to be successful.

Understanding the Foundation of Big Data

Big data techniques are designed to manage a huge volume of disparate data at the right speed and within the right time frame. The goal is to enable near real-time analysis and action. Four characters typically define big data: Volume (how much data), Validity (correctness and accuracy based on intended use), Velocity (how fast that data is ingested and processed), and Veracity (the truthfulness of the data to solve a problem). The key issues that are important to understand are how much data you have and how much you need. You need to understand how fast that data needs to be processed based on the problem you need to solve. Finally, you need to consider the various types of data that will ensure that you are making well-informed decisions. In this section, we will delve into the different types of data that we need to work with in order to be prepared for augmented intelligence.

To gain the type of insights into data that we need to be able make more informed decisions requires enough data so that results are trustworthy. Data of all forms need to be mapped and understood in context. Data is only getting more complicated, with more nuances than ever. How do you map highly structured data with highly unstructured data such as written material, video and images? How do you ensure that there aren't biases within your data sets? How can you pre-train data so that it is easier to get predictable results? All of these questions are fundamental to being able to augment our ability to use advanced analytics to make better decisions. Before we discuss the details of how companies are making the transition from big data to AI and augmented intelligence, we need to start with the basics. We divide the foundations of big data into three types: structured, unstructured, and semi-structured data.

Structured versus Unstructured Data

Structured data refers to information that has a defined length and format—for example, numbers, dates, and names. A majority of traditional business applications are designed to manage highly structured data. The traditional relational database was structured so that each element was defined, including the relationships within the data sets. This structure made it possible to create understandable answers to questions inside this data.

The initial use cases of structured data were used to coming up with answers to relatively straightforward questions. However, questions have become increasingly more complicated as devices generate more and more data (such as sensor data), and companies create data resulting from human interactions with computers. Data generated by data logs, point-of-sale data, and clickstream data are often referred to as semi-structured data. Machine learning models are well suited to the structure and tagging of structured data.

For most of the history of the computer industry, the focus has been on structured data. However, this has begun to change dramatically over the past decade as we have discovered new ways of gaining insights from data without traditional structure. Over time, we have moved from the ability to analyze basic text to now being able to leverage unstructured data in new ways. Increasingly, we are able to add structure and nuance to unstructured data in order to gain an understanding of meaning buried in complex documents, as well as text, videos, images, atmospheric data, voice, and social media. Clearly, being able to understand the content and context of unstructured data is imperative for machine learning and, specifically, augmented intelligence.

Unstructured data does not have a predefined data model nor is it organized in a predefined manner. Therefore, it is not surprising that most of the information in the world is unstructured. Unstructured information is typically text-heavy, but it may contain data such as dates, numbers, and facts as well. This results in irregularities and ambiguities that make it difficult to understand using traditional programs as compared to data stored in fielded form in databases or annotated (semantically tagged) in documents.

Despite the abundance of unstructured data, machine learning algorithms don't work well without structure. Of course, there is inherent structure even in unstructured data, but the difference is that humans have to do the hard work to understand the hidden structure of the data. Therefore, for unstructured data to work well in machine learning, you have to be able to understand the features and attributes of the data.

Turning unstructured data into meaningful information can be much more complex than dealing with the highly structured databases. In reality, there is no such thing as data without any structure. The imperative for finding meaning in unstructured data is to understand the hidden patterns within that data. This is the technique that is the foundation of Natural Language Processing, which derives an understanding of what a collection of words means based on understanding usage patterns.

Machine Learning Techniques

You need to understand the fundamentals of machine learning techniques in order to understand how far these algorithms and models will take you. We will discuss building models in depth in Chapter 4.

Dealing with Constraints

The availability of massive amounts of data that can be stored and processed at incredible speeds is imperative to success with machine learning. However, there are constraints that make it difficult to get to the results that help a business achieve the type of breakthroughs that can set it apart from the competition. First, what is the nature of the data? What is the source of that data? Is the data reliable and is it the right data to solve the problem? Is there enough expertise within the data science team? The smartest data scientists are of little value if they don't understand the business problem they have been asked to solve. These scientists may do a wonderful job selecting a good algorithm and preparing data, but they may not have good intuition about critical business problems. To be successful, the data scientist must be able to collaborate with "subject matter experts," that is, business experts.

Therefore, before even working with the data, it is important to understand the business process. Why focus first on business process? Simply put, anything that is achieved in business must be based on a process for solving a problem. For example, are you trying to create a new process to better maintain machinery on the factory floor based on the data that machines generate? What is the optimal process for ensuring safety and efficient production? In diagnosing a disease, what is the process needed to support a doctor's ability to understand both individual patients and their history, and to apply the accumulated knowledge of successful treatment outcomes to their symptoms? We include the details of business process in Chapter 3.

Once you understand the processes you are dealing with, you now have to understand how to prepare and manage the data so that it is helpful in solving problems. Data has to be tagged to enable machine learning. For example, "chicken" can mean an animal or it could be the first word in "chicken pox"—very different meanings although the word is identical. Tagging is one of the most complex issues that has to be solved when organizations are using a massive amount of data to understand the best next step. When you are dealing with a small data set, it is possible to have a human tag data so that the machine and the algorithms understand it. For example, using the chicken pox example, the subject matter expert can tag data based on the knowledge of the disease. There are often commercial data sets available that are pre-tagged. They will understand what terms mean and tag them so that the data can be accurately processed and provide answers and conclusions. But what happens if you are dealing with a massive amount of data that is untagged? In this case, you need to be able to apply methods that can anticipate what the tags might be. Automating the tagging process is one of the emerging innovations that will support the maturation of artificial intelligence. This automatic tagging is essential to help a data scientist build algorithms to support decision making.

Without the innovations in the field of advanced analytics over the past decade, augmented intelligence would not be possible. In the second half of the last century, tremendous progress was made through the growth in computing hardware systems. The industry evolved from a handful of vendors producing extremely expensive, massive systems only accessible to a few to smaller computer systems that were affordable to even the smallest business unit. Despite the fact that incredible progress was being made, the performance and capability of these early systems paled in comparison to what we see today. Because of the limitations in computer memory, computing performance, networking speeds, and data movement, the tasks that could be performed by technology were limited.

Smart technologists found ingenious ways to squeeze as much performance as possible out of limited resources. Relational databases provided a pragmatic way to analyze data in an accessible way to the massive number of businesses that wanted to begin analyzing the data that they housed in their systems. Data is not straightforward—especially when you move out of the world of highly structured databases. The traditional relational database was developed in an era when compute power and data storage were extremely expensive. Therefore, databases had to be optimized to collect data efficiently and provide business users with a clear way of getting answers to questions.

Several different technology advances make augmented intelligence feasible today. First, there have been advances in machine learning techniques that make it possible to leverage the insights captured in data. These advances have been combined with scalable infrastructure in the cloud that makes it possible to store up to petabytes of data, coupled with powerful compute engines that can drive the advanced analytics to gain insights from the data. Second, the rise of big data means a rise in data volumes and diversity. The net effect is that there is more data available from both structured and unstructured sources, along with techniques to integrate and analyze these diverse sources.

Understanding Machine Learning

Machine learning and AI are emerging as the answer to many of the complex business problems being addressed by advanced analytics. There is a presumption that if you simply apply machine learning algorithms to a problem, you will gain insights that were never possible in the past. There is no debate that existing business leaders are facing new and unanticipated competitors. These businesses are looking at new strategies that can prepare them for the future. Although there are many different strategies that a business can try, they all come back to a fundamental truth—you have to follow the data. And you need to ensure that you are using the right data with the right techniques to achieve your results.

What Is Machine Learning?

Machine learning has become one of the most important topics within development organizations that are looking for innovative ways to leverage data assets to help the business gain a new level of understanding. Why add machine learning into the mix? With the appropriate machine learning models, organizations have the ability to continually predict changes in the business so that they are best able to predict what's next. As data is constantly added, the machine learning models ensure that the solution is constantly updated. The value is straightforward: If you use the most appropriate and constantly changing data sources in the context of machine learning, you have the opportunity to predict the future.

Machine learning is a form of artificial intelligence that enables a system to learn from data rather than through explicit programming of a set of rules.

Machine learning algorithms themselves learn to divide each data observation into a category. Categories can be very varied. They can consist of a group of faces associated to a particular person's name or the set of choices of what products to show a customer. However, machine learning is not a simple process.

Machine learning consists of a variety of types of algorithms, all of which iteratively learn from data to improve, describe data, and predict outcomes. As the algorithms ingest training data, they result in a model (a set of categories which form its predictions) for that data. It is then possible to use that model on new data that the machine learning algorithm has not seen before to make more predictions. A machine learning model is the output generated when you train your machine learning algorithm with data. After training, when you provide the model with new data input, its output will be provide new insights regarding the data.

You likely interact with machine learning applications without realizing it. For example, when you visit an e-commerce site and start viewing products and reading reviews, you will likely be presented with other, similar products that you might find interesting. These recommendations are not hard coded by an army of developers. The suggestions are served to the site via a machine learning model. The model ingests your browsing history along with other shoppers' browsing and purchasing data in order to present other similar products that you might want to purchase.

Iterative Learning from Data

Machine learning enables models to train on data sets before being deployed. Some machine learning models are online and continuously adapt as new data is ingested. On the other hand, other models—known as offline machine learning models—are derived from machine learning algorithms, but once deployed, do not change. This iterative process of online models leads to an improvement in the types of associations that are made between data elements. Due to their complexity and size, these patterns and associations could have easily been overlooked by human observation. Once a model has been trained, these models can be used in real time to learn from data. Offline models do not have this advantage and must be retrained periodically with new data.

In addition, complex algorithms can be automatically adjusted based on rapid changes in variables such as sensor data, time, weather data, and customer sentiment metrics. For example, inferences can be made from a machine learning model: If the weather changes quickly, a weather predicting model can predict a tornado, and a warning siren can be triggered. The improvements in accuracy are a result of the training process and automation that is part of machine learning. Online machine learning algorithms continuously refine the models by continually processing new data in near real time and training the system to adapt to changing patterns and associations in the data.

One of the innovations that has made a significant contribution to the acceleration of machine learning is the open source community. As a consequence, there are more resources, frameworks, and libraries that have made development easier. These open source communities result from 40 years of research by scientists to invent ML algorithms and create data sets using them. Although companies also invent new ML algorithms that they do not share, many new algorithms are shared because scientists recognize the value in sharing scientific discoveries. The scientific community in universities has invented and made publically available most of the vast collection of ML algorithms. The business community should thank them for their work as well as organizations such as the National Science Foundation, the National Institutes of Health, and the Department of Defense (DoD), which have sponsored research at universities in the United States to invent and understand machine learning.

The Roles of Statistics and Data Mining in Machine Learning

The disciplines of statistics, data mining, and machine learning all have a role in understanding data and describing the characteristics of a data set as well as finding relationships and patterns in that data and building a model. There is a great deal of overlap in how the techniques and tools of these disciplines are applied to solving business problems.

Many of the widely used data mining and machine learning algorithms are rooted in classical statistical analysis. Data scientists combine technology backgrounds with expertise in statistics, data mining, and machine learning to use all disciplines collaboratively. Regardless of the combination of capabilities and technology used to predict outcomes, having an understanding of the business problem and business goals, as well as subject matter expertise, is essential. You can't expect to get good results by focusing on the statistics alone, without considering the business side to pick critical business problems to solve.

The following highlights how these capabilities relate to each other. Machine learning algorithms are covered in the next section in greater detail due to the importance of this discipline to advanced analytics.

Statistics is the science of analyzing the data. Classical or conventional statistics is inferential in nature, meaning it is used to reach conclusions about the data (various parameters). Statistical modeling is focused primarily on making inferences and understanding the characteristics of the variables. Machine learning provide a way to computationally encode various statistical techniques. Data scientists take statistical ideas and encode them as algorithms and then apply those algorithms to data to make predictions.

Putting Machine Learning in Context

To understand the role of machine learning, let's start with some context. Artificial intelligence, machine learning, and deep learning are all terms that are frequently mentioned when discussing big data, analytics, and advanced technology. Artificial intelligence seeks to understand the mechanisms underlying thought and intelligent behavior. AI includes the subfields of natural language processing, vision, robotics, machine learning, and knowledge representation and reasoning. Machine learning is the sub-field that focuses on theories and algorithms to make it possible for a machine to learn a task or to make a prediction. A machine that can translate a paragraph of English into another language uses AI (both machine learning and natural language processing), and a thermostat that learns your preferences for keeping your home comfortable uses machine learning.

Approaches to Machine Learning

Depending on the nature of the business problem being addressed, there are different approaches based on the type and volume of the data. There are a number of approaches to machine learning that are relevant to the ability to create algorithms that support business problems. These approaches contain two main types: supervised learning and unsupervised learning. Two often-discussed types of unsupervised learning are reinforcement learning and deep learning.

Supervised Learning

Supervised learning typically begins with an established set of data that has been classified manually. The algorithm builds a model to match the inputs and outputs of the data. Supervised learning is intended to find patterns in data that can be applied to an analytics process. This data has labeled features or is data that has been enhanced with a tag or label that describes its category or use. Because the attributes of the data have been identified, training the data should produce a model with reliable outputs. An example of supervised learning is weather forecasting. Using supervised learning, weather forecasting takes into account known historical weather patterns and the current conditions to provide a prediction about the weather.

When supervised algorithms are trained using preprocessed examples, the resulting model must be evaluated against test data to see how well it learned. Occasionally, patterns that are identified in a subset of the data can't be detected in the larger population of data. If the model is fit to only represent the patterns that exist in the training subset, the problem called overfitting occurs. Overfitting means that your model is precisely tuned for your training data but may not be applicable for large sets of unknown data. To protect against overfitting, testing needs to be done against unforeseen or unknown labeled data. Using unforeseen data for the test set can help you evaluate the accuracy of the model in predicting outcomes and results.

Unsupervised Learning

Unsupervised learning is best suited when the problem requires a massive amount of data that is unlabeled. For example, social media applications such as Twitter, Instagram, Snapchat, etc., all have large amounts of unlabeled data. To understand the meaning behind this data requires algorithms that can begin to understand the meaning based on being able to classify the data based on the patterns or clusters it finds. Therefore, the unsupervised learning algorithm conducts an iterative process of analyzing data without human intervention. Unsupervised learning is used in many applications including email spam–detecting technology. There are far too many variables in legitimate and spam emails for an analyst to flag unsolicited bulk email. Instead, machine learning classifiers based on clustering and association are applied in order to identify unwanted email.

Unsupervised learning algorithms segment data into groups of examples (clusters) or groups of features. The unlabeled data creates the parameter values and classification of the data. In essence, this process adds labels to the data so that it becomes supervised. Unsupervised learning can determine the outcome when there is a massive amount of data. In this case, the developer doesn't know the context of the data being analyzed, so labeling is not possible at this stage. Therefore, unsupervised learning can be used as the first step before passing the data to a supervised learning process.

Unsupervised learning algorithms can help businesses understand large volumes of new, unlabeled data. Similar to supervised learning, these algorithms look for patterns in the data; however, the difference is that the data is not already understood. For example, in healthcare, collecting huge amounts of data about a specific disease can help practitioners gain insights into the patterns of symptoms and relate those to outcomes for patients. It would take too much time to label all of the data sources associated with a disease such as diabetes. Therefore, an unsupervised learning approach with help determine outcomes more quickly than a supervised learning approach.

Reinforcement Learning

Reinforcement learning is a behavioral learning model. The algorithm receives feedback from the analysis of the data so that the user is guided to the best outcome. Reinforcement learning differs from other types of supervised learning because the system receives ongoing positive and negative rewards as it makes decisions using the data. In short, a reinforcement learning system learns through trial and error. Therefore, a sequence of successful decisions will result in the process being "reinforced" because it best solves the problem at hand.

One of the most common applications of reinforcement learning is in robotics or game playing. Take the example of the need to train a robot to navigate a set of stairs. The robot changes its approach to navigating the terrain based on the outcome of its actions. When the robot falls, the data is recalibrated so that the steps are navigated differently until the robot is trained by trial and error to understand how to climb stairs. In other words, the robot learns based on a successful sequence of actions. The learning algorithm has to be able to discover an association between the goal of climbing stairs successfully without falling and the sequence of events that lead to the outcome.

Neural Networks and Deep Learning

Deep learning is a specific method of machine learning that incorporates neural networks in successive layers in order to learn from data in an iterative manner. Deep learning is especially useful when you are trying to learn patterns from unstructured data.

Deep learning and related complex neural networks are designed to emulate how the human brain works so that computers can be trained to deal with abstractions and problems that are poorly defined. The average five-year-old child can easily recognize the difference between his teacher's face and the face of the crossing guard. In contrast, the computer has to do a lot of work to figure out who is who. Neural networks and deep learning are often used in image recognition, speech, and computer vision applications.

A neural network consists of three or more layers: an input layer, one or many hidden layers, and an output layer. Data is ingested through the input layer. Weights on the nodes in the hidden layers are adjusted until data is output at the output layer. The typical neural network may consist of thousands or even millions of simple processing nodes that are densely interconnected. The term deep learning is used when there are multiple hidden layers within a neural network. Using an iterative approach, a neural network continuously adjusts and makes inferences until a specific stopping point is reached.

Evolving to Deep Learning

There are many areas in which deep learning will have an impact on businesses. For example, voice recognition will have applications in everything from automobiles to customer management. For Internet of Things (IoT) manufacturing applications, deep learning can be used to predict when a machine will malfunction. Deep learning algorithms can help law enforcement personnel keep track of the movements of a known suspect.

Preparing for Augmented Intelligence

It is clear that infrastructure—both in terms of cloud, data, and machine learning—comprises the building blocks for making artificial intelligence a reality. Cloud services provide the elasticity, scalability, and price/performance needed to manage the massive amount of data needed to gain insights into complex data models. However, without the ability to prepare data so that it is clean and accurate, it is not possible to gain significant insights into the data that is the foundation of augmented intelligence. When you combine cloud services with data management, you are now in a good position to put machine learning models to use to significantly improve our ability to gain insights and take action.

Chapter 3

The Cycle of Data

Introduction

One of the most significant challenges to succeeding with augmented intelligence is the need to consistently manage data so that it can be applied to critical business problems. Many companies make the mistake of selecting a data source without doing the hard work of getting the data ready for use. There is a cycle of managing data that begins with data acquisition, moves on to data preparation, and progresses to the building of a predictive model based on the data. Data is needed to build and test the predictive models that are core to augmented intelligence. The work then cycles back to data acquisition in support of model improvement and ongoing model maintenance.

As we discussed in Chapter 2, we have made the movement from the traditional database model to a big data focus driven by the revolutions happening in infrastructure. The transition from traditional analytics to augmented intelligence requires a foundation of big data as part of the journey. You can't simply move from a traditional packaged application and a relational database to augmented intelligence.

Traditional business applications and data management practices cannot support augmented intelligence. What are the traditional business applications currently in use in most organizations? These applications fall into two broad categories: transactional applications, which capture operational data such as customer orders or claims, and reporting applications that keep track of how well a business performed in the past, such as sales by product line and profit and loss. By contrast, augmented intelligence relies on predictive analytics intended to discover patterns in historical data so that this data can be used to predict the future.

How are predictive applications different from traditional business applications? The most important aspect of a predictive application is that it provides a technique to guide decision making. Predicting future events is much more complex than simply reporting on what has already taken place. The only way to truly begin to understand where your business is headed is to leverage a vast array of data from both inside and outside of the company. The analysis of such a rich data set via machine intelligence enables the data scientist to discover patterns in earlier business events that enable them to predict future outcomes. This knowledge provides guidance on the course of action the data scientist should take that will likely yield the best result. An action can be generated automatically by the machine learning algorithm if the process itself is straightforward. On the other hand, complex decision making will require that the machine learning process provide guidance to decision makers.

The use of machine learning algorithms for predictive analytics is powerful and can be used for both collaboration and knowledge transfer and personalization. The bottom line is that there are multiple techniques for leveraging machine learning to enhance the ability for businesses to solve complex problems. What is the difference between a collaborative approach and personalization?

Knowledge Transfer

Knowledge transfer across an organization is essential to the success of every organization. Knowing how the best performers use data to get work done is especially valuable. Such knowledge can make a junior employee more productive. For example, an experienced sales representative knows when to continue to nurture a lead and when to move on, based on a customer's response to actions taken in the sales process. Providing predictive model-guided recommendations to a junior sales representative on the next best action to take in pursuing a lead is an effective means of knowledge transfer.

Personalization

Machine intelligence allows businesses to deliver a personalized experience to customers, employees, and suppliers. This personalization is based on an analysis of data on each person's communication style and preferences. The success of a personalized communication strategy depends on the development of compelling content and the delivery of the content at the right time to the right individual. Businesses use models that predict likely customer response to identify what content to deliver to each customer and when the delivery should take place.

Determining the Right Data for Building Models

Simply put, you must have the appropriate data and the right amount of data to build predictive models. But as we mentioned in Chapter 2, it is not enough to simply apply data to creating a model. You have to begin by establishing the "training data set." In many cases, the most common type of machine learning is supervised learning. The training data provides examples of input data (the independent variables) and output data (the dependent or target variable). Supervised learning seeks to infer a function between the input variables and the target variable we seek to predict. The resulting function or model is then tested on new data (called the "test data set"). The test data has the same structure as the training data, containing the same input features and the target feature (the correct answer). The accuracy of the function in predicting the target feature is evaluated. Several iterations of training, building, and testing follow.

The success of the model-building process depends on the quality, breadth, and relevance of the data used to train and test the model. Consider, for example, a data set related to real estate. There are records for each property that contain features about the property. These features include the property identifier, lot size, house size, number of rooms, location, and taxes billed. There are also related records of sales transactions for properties. The sales transaction records contain the property identifier as a link to the property records, along with features for buyer, seller, mortgage supplier, transaction date, and selling price. The property records and sales transaction records are merged using the property identifier feature that is common to both sets of records.

The merged data set (real estate data) is the source of candidate features for the development of a model to predict the current market value of the property. For a model to predict real estate prices, features in the real estate data set such as lot size, interior space in the house, number of rooms, and location are potential input features for the function expressed by the model. The target feature is the actual sales price, as recorded in the property sales transaction records.

The Phases of the Data Cycle

Figure 3-1 illustrates the three phases of the data cycle in support of the development of a predictive model which includes acquiring the data, preparing the data, and using the data to build the predictive model.

The three phases of the data cycle form an iterative feedback loop:

- **Data acquisition:** Some of the data needed for model building may already exist within an organization. Other data to supplement the internal data

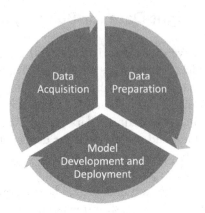

Figure 3-1   The Data Cycle

can be acquired. This data may include product lists, order transactions, and equipment maintenance records. Unstructured data such as best practice documents, history, and regulations are also important for context and understanding. Data management specialists within the IT or corporate data function load data sets into a shared resource to be drawn upon for a range of modeling projects across business groups. Line of business (LOB) data scientists and business analysts may seek to acquire supplementary data, as needed, for specific modeling projects. Before the supplementary data may be used, permissions must be obtained from data owners.

- **Data preparation:** Data scientists and LOB analysts explore relevant data sets and their relationships to one another. The exploration uncovers errors and anomalies that must be addressed in a process known as data cleansing. Then the features or attributes of the data are examined for the purpose of selecting the input variables with the best chance of predicting the target feature. Features are added or subtracted to aid in the development of the model. This step is called "feature engineering."

- **Model development and deployment:** With the help of domain experts, data scientists build and test predictive models using statistical and machine learning techniques. Based on the preliminary testing results, feature engineering may resume in an effort to improve the model's capability to generate accurate predictions of the target variable. When testing shows that the model has achieved an acceptable level of accuracy, the model is ready for deployment. While in use, the model's operational performance and accuracy continues to be monitored.

- **Back to acquisition:** Based on ongoing testing and evaluation of the model, additional data may be needed in order to improve the accuracy of the model's predictions. This need for additional data triggers a new round of data acquisition. Thus, the data cycle continues: returning to data acquisition, followed by data preparation, then to model maintenance and redevelopment.

Each of these aspects of the data cycle is complex and requires explanation. In this next section, we will delve into each aspect of the cycle and explore the nuances required.

Data Acquisition

To build a new predictive model, a business needs good data. To gain competitive advantage, a business must leverage the data it already possesses and acquire supplementary data, as needed, for model development. To be successful, it is mandatory to understand the details of all of your existing data, including its origin and usage. It is also critical to understand what information is missing. Once your organization collects all of the data required, you are ready to prepare your data for building models.

Identifying Data Already within the Organization

Businesses capture data about their products and customers during ongoing operations. Yet in some cases, teams may not realize that the organization already possesses a tremendous amount of data and knowledge. Often a business's organizational structure may work against the ability and willingness of groups to share data. One of the consequences of this isolation is that decisions can be made without the proper context. Smart business leaders understand the value of learning from data across the company.

Consider the following situation at an international cruise line. Marketing operations within the cruise line were divided between two groups. One group was responsible for marketing the daily excursions offered during a cruise, while another group was responsible for marketing the cruises themselves. The marketing team responsible for promoting excursions during a cruise was proud of a new program for marketing daily excursions to customers while they were on a cruise.

Here is how the program worked. Each day, every customer received a personalized communication in the form of a custom newsletter left under the door of his or her cabin describing the excursions available that day. The featured excursions took account of individual cruisegoer preferences identified by the predictive model. The delivery of personalized communications to cruise passengers on the day excursions were offered resulted in a significant increase in daily sales.

That was an excellent outcome for the cruise line. But this data on customer preferences for activities during a cruise was valuable for other marketing activities as well. Specifically, information about the excursions a customer preferred would also help marketers identify which future cruise the customer might enjoy. The marketing team could then target potential customers for cruises that featured the types of activities they had selected for daily excursions. Yet the data on excursion preferences during a cruise was not part of the customer data sets used by the group responsible for marketing the cruises. Additionally, correspondence and reviews of excursions could also help to ensure that marketers understood what changes could improve their offerings. Eventually, management recognized that combining the customer excursion and customer cruise data could result in increased revenue across both organizations.

Once management mandated that the two organizations should collaborate, the two data sets were combined. The resulting merged data sets yielded better insights on customer preferences, both for cruises and for cruise excursions. Each group improved its marketing outcomes by leveraging the expanded, enriched data. The new information on customer preferences was shared with travel professionals so that they could offer customers new cruise packages that helped to drive additional incremental revenue.

Reasons for Acquiring Additional Data

Sometimes, not all of the required data is currently available within the organization. In that case, the company may need to collect additional data. For example, industrial companies with big capital investments in heavy equipment are investing in the development of models that predict when the equipment is likely to fail. With the predictions, a company can intervene to repair the equipment before it fails. But before the models can be built, new sensors must be installed on the equipment to acquire data on the performance of the equipment. Analysis of the sensor data integrated with other data about the equipment previously acquired enables the discovery of patterns that predict either continued normal operations or the likelihood of specific types of equipment failure. The prediction of a type of imminent failure leads to a recommendation of the specific repair needed to avert the failure.

In other situations, organizations may need to collect data aggregated from outside sources. When a model's training data is limited to data captured within the organization, there is a risk of perpetuating an organization's biases. Therefore, external data may help avoid unintended biases. For example, if a data scientist builds a candidate-selection model based solely on data regarding the performance of current employees, the model is likely to be biased. Training a model based on attributes similar to the successful employees may result in discriminatory hiring practices by missing good candidates who are different from those already in the organization. Discriminatory hiring practices can dramatically hurt a company's reputation and can result in legal liability. A more broad set that includes outside data can address such problems. Professional associations, Internet employment sites, or government agencies have data on the attributes of people in particular occupations across an industry or across multiple firms. These sources can provide data on candidates with attributes different from the company's current employees.

Consider the demographics of a major symphony orchestra from 50 years ago. White male hiring managers employed musicians who were like them. It was uncommon for women or people of color to be hired. How has this practice evolved? Many orchestras introduced blind auditions into the hiring process. The revised process required hiring managers to judge candidates who auditioned from behind a curtain. Judges had no knowledge of the gender or race of the candidate while they listened to his or her musical performance. This single process modification resulted in a far more varied population of musicians, and, arguably, a higher quality of overall orchestra performance. Data collected on employees across symphony orchestras today would yield a far more diverse data set. Predictive models trained on this data would not be limited by the biased hiring policies of the past.

These examples show that it's not the sheer quantity of data that makes for the best training data set. A data set, even if quite large, may be homogeneous and incorporate the same limitations. Protecting the model from inherent bias depends on the richness and diversity of the data. Data variety can be more important than data volume for successful training of a predictive model.

Data Preparation

Once the data is acquired, it must be prepared. Data preparation requires an organizational commitment to the ongoing management of the data cycle that includes all of the key constituents, including data professionals, LOB application specialists, subject matter experts, and business analysts. Preparation improves the quality of the data used to train predictive models. Analytics and model building are actually only about 20% of the effort. Data preparation is where as much as 80% of the work is accomplished. Good data preparation is very challenging for the following reasons:

- **Labor intensive:** There are many data tasks that are extremely labor intensive. In some cases, employees are required to input the same data into multiple applications. This leads to errors, wasted time, and added costs. Automation based on machine learning models is beginning to be used to reduce these errors and costs.

- **Relevance and context:** It are common for an organization to collect data sources that seem logical, only to discover that the context is not correct. Sometimes the data source that seems relevant may be out of date. In other situations, the data source may include sensitive data that cannot be shared.

- **Complexity:** It used to be the case that analytics and model buildings were based entirely on structured data. This data is typically predefined and, therefore, simpler to access. But with the advent of big data, organizations need to be able to leverage multiple types of data. Data may be in the form of images, text, or sound, where the structure has not been predefined. This type of data requires preprocessing to learn its actual structure so that the data can be analyzed in context. For example, later in this chapter, a case study shows how an online travel aggregator derives additional features about locations (hotels, restaurants, tours, etc.) by analyzing the language in user reviews. This new information then can be blended in with data about these same entities found in the structured data sources to yield an enriched data set.

- **Anomalies:** Separate data sets may contain data on the same suppliers or customers. But the suppliers or customers may be referred to by different names or have different identifiers. These anomalies must be resolved before data on entities from separately maintained sources can be merged. There can also be missing values for specific data features that must be resolved in a consistent way across the data sources.

Data preparation has traditionally been the domain of data management professionals. However, it is equally important to include business analysts who have specific domain knowledge to evaluate data sources for potential use in their LOB. Today, new self-service methods of data cleansing are available for use by LOB specialists to participate in the data preparation process. The following case study of data preparation used a self-service ("data wrangling") approach to address data anomalies. A key issue to resolve was missing data on defendants and co-defendants, which made it difficult to meet a court mandate to identify people who were convicted based on falsified drug tests. This issue of falsified drug tests is discussed in more detail in the box on the next page.

Preparing Data for Machine Learning and AI

One of the most important issues in the cycle of data is to make sure that you have selected the right data sources that are prepared in the correct manner that produces the right results. One of the greatest dangers is that an analyst grabs data sources that are inaccurate. The consequences can be dire if your

---

Case Study: Data Wrangling and the Law[1-3]

Annie Dookhan, a chemist at the William A. Hinton State Laboratory Institute in Boston, was responsible for testing drug samples seized by police—evidence for prosecuting defendants charged with drug offenses. She confessed to tampering with the evidence, forging test results, and lying about her activities. The state's highest court ordered that a list be produced of the defendants impacted by Ms. Dookhan's actions. But the creation of the list was a challenge. The main data source was the receipt of drugs by the lab. But there were quality problems in this data source:

- The receipts contained no docket numbers to tie the data to a specific case.
- There was not always sufficient space to include all the co-defendants for a case.
- With no personal identifiers other than names on the receipts, it wasn't clear whether multiple occurrences of common names like "John Smith" or "Carlos Gomez" in the data set referred to different people or the same person.

To improve the list of defendants impacted by the lab scandal, other data sources were needed. One useful source turned out to be police reports, which often had names of co-defendants. Other sources were the files of staff attorneys who handled the cases and had names of all the co-defendants for a case. Lawyers with skills in data preparation techniques examined police reports to determine whether there were additional co-defendants that were not included in the drug receipts. Then they used several open source Python algorithms to match the list of defendants from the drug receipt data with the defendants in the case files.

In the end, an improved list was submitted to the court, and over 20,000 cases were dismissed. Many defendants were freed, and only a few hundred of the cases were set aside for re-prosecution. The application of data science to load, clean, and merge related data sets ("data wrangling") improved the accuracy of the list of defendants and co-defendants who were impacted by the tainted drug tests. Complying with the court's mandate to develop the list required a combination of legal and data technology expertise.

organization is using the analytics to predict which direction to take your products and services. So, how do you make sure that you are preparing your data to support advanced machine learning and artificial intelligence (AI). There are three major steps in data preparation:

- Data exploration
- Data cleansing
- Feature engineering

Data Exploration

Before beginning data preparation, it is imperative to gain an understanding of the data. To get started, it is imperative to be able to explore the data that seems to be pertinent to the problem your organization is trying to solve. Data scientists and business analysts need to become familiar with the features of the data. This exploration will reveal the relationships among the data sets so they can potentially be merged. Analysts also need to gain insights into the correctness of the data. There may be errors and anomalies that will impact results. This exploration will identify which features appear to have the greatest impact on the dependent variable—the result that the model seeks to predict.

Data exploration seeks to answer the following questions:

- What are the available features within the data?
- Is the data complete, or are there a lot of missing values?
- Are there features that are correlated with each other?
- What is the correlation of individual features with the target variable?

Data Cleansing

Once errors and anomalies in the data have been identified in data exploration, they can be managed through a process known as data cleansing. This phase seeks to remediate the errors and anomalies that have been discovered. Data cleansing requires strategies for the handling of missing values and resolving inconsistencies in data features to identify entities. These identifiers are required to link separate data sets together on the same subject. The work can be partially automated via machine learning algorithms that use pattern-matching techniques. However, subject matter experts must be involved to ensure that the correct data is being ingested into the model.

To understand the relationship between data exploration and data cleansing, consider the issues of missing values and inconsistent values. These anomalies are discovered in data exploration and addressed in data cleansing:

- **Missing values:** Some records may be missing values for various features or fields. A quick fix for missing values in a field is to average out all of the present values in a data set for a field and then rely on this average or mean value to replace each missing value for that feature. But this method is overly simplistic and may not yield the best results. Machine learning algorithms can examine patterns in the other fields of a record in order to derive a better estimate. For example, if the value of the total interior size of a house is missing, data on the number of rooms can be used to derive a better estimate. An even better estimate might combine data on the number of rooms with data on the age of the house—since room size tends to vary depending on when the house was built. Location data (such as zip code/postal code) can also be factored in, as homes in certain geographic areas tend to have larger rooms than homes in other areas.
- **Inconsistent values:** There may be inconsistent values for fields, which prevents the merging of data from multiple sources about a single entity. For example, the same company may have different names across data sets, or even within the same data set. For example, "IBM," "International Business Machines," and "IBM, Inc." all refer to the same entity. Machine learning algorithms can detect inconsistencies in the data and then address the problem by mapping the different names to a single entity name. Human domain specialists then can review this work and flag false matches. The algorithm learns from this feedback and applies a modified strategy on the next round. Over time, the matching algorithm improves, resulting in a reduced percentage of false matches.

To see how data exploration and data cleansing operate together in practice, we'll examine the data preparation strategies used by entrants in the Zillow competition to build a model to predict housing prices. Zillow, the popular real estate site, recently conducted an open contest for improving their Z-estimate model that assigns a market value to 110 million homes in the United States. The individual data science competitors were provided a real estate data set on the Kaggle website (a platform established as a platform for competitions among data science teams).[4] The data had been merged from the multiple sources that Zillow uses for its Zestimate model. Zillow described the sources of the data it uses for calculating its Zestimates:

> *To calculate the Zestimate home valuation, Zillow uses data from county and tax assessor records, and direct feeds from hundreds of multiple listing services and brokerages. Additionally, homeowners have the ability to update facts about their homes, which may result in a change to their Zestimate.*[5,6]

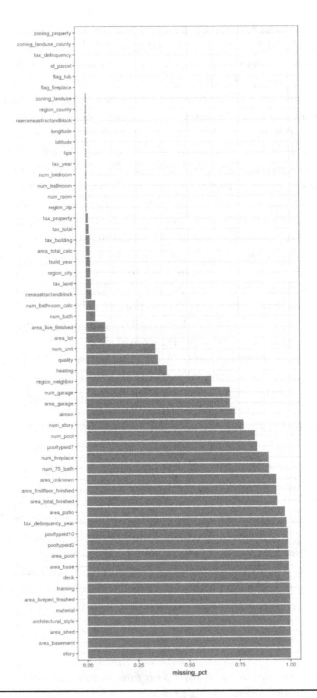

Figure 3-2 Zillow/Kaggle Competition: Features with Highest Percentage of Missing Values (*Source:* Kaggle, Exploratory Analysis, Zillow[7])

Contestants were then tasked with predicting the log of the error between the Z-estimate value and the actual sale price for the property. Zillow claimed that prior to the competition their Z-estimate had improved to within 5% of the actual price.

Several entrants in the Zillow competition documented how they explored the data provided on the Kaggle site and the strategies they used to deal with the anomalies they found. The first challenge they faced was the 56 features in the property data set. That's an unwieldy number of features to evaluate as candidate predictors of property value.

The second major challenge was the large percentage of missing values, which impacted data quality. Figure 3-2 shows a visualization of the features in the Zillow/Kaggle data set with the highest percentage of missing values. The features are ordered in ascending order according to percentage of missing values.

Based on what you've learned about the data set, you may decide to delete the features with the greatest percentage of missing values—for example, those with >75% missing value. Alternatively, you could look to estimate values that are missing when there is a high correlation between two variables.

For example, further data exploration reveals that the bedroom-count feature turns out to be highly correlated with the bathroom-count feature. That makes sense, since a house with fewer bedrooms would logically require fewer bathrooms. You could develop a function to express the relationship between the two features. Using this approach, you could calculate the value of the of the feature with the missing value based on the feature where the value is present. You could also create a new feature—total-room-count—adding the values of bedroom-count and bathroom-count together. Figure 3-3 shows the correlation between different features. The larger and darker circles indicate a stronger correlation.

Deciding on which features to keep, which to delete, and which to create is the process of feature engineering. Here is where you apply the learning gained in data exploration in order to upgrade the quality of the data available for predictive model development.

Feature Engineering

Feature engineering is the refining of the features on the data set for use in predictive model development via a process of feature selection and feature creation. Feature engineering is an art that requires domain knowledge, data skills, and creativity to be performed effectively.

There are several approaches to feature engineering in which you prepare the data set for predictive model development.

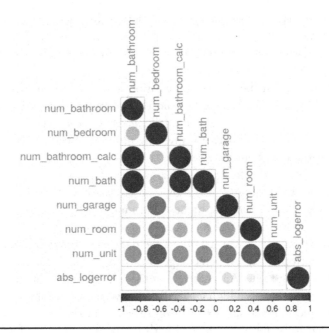

Figure 3-3 Zillow/Kaggle Competition: Correlation Across Features (*Source: Kaggle, Exploratory Analysis, Zillow*[7])

- **Feature selection:** You decide which features to delete and which to retain in a data set, applying the learning from data exploration and your knowledge about the domain of the prediction you are trying to build. For example, as noted in the last section, you could decide to delete those features with a high percentage of missing values, only retaining those features with a low percentage of missing values.
- **Feature creation:** You can derive new features out of the existing data via various methods of calculation, binning, or extraction.
  - **Feature creation via calculation:** For example, we noted in the last section that a new feature—total-room-count—could be derived by adding together the values for the count of bedrooms and the count of bathrooms. The new feature had fewer missing values than either of the two original features. Another example is zip code and Federal Information Processing Standard (FIPS) code, both indicators of geographic location. Combining these two features into a new feature could reduce the percentage of missing values as compared to either feature alone.

○ **Feature creation via binning:** Classifying feature values into a category use a technique known as statistical data binning (a way to group data about a specific like value). This is useful for numeric values in a continuous range. You could group people via their age into millennials, gen-Xers, or baby boomers by specifying a beginning and an ending birth date. This groups values from a date or number into a category with a limited set of possible values. Another form of binning is used in finance to group accounts in aging categories—accounts less than 30 days old, 30–60 days old, and so on.

- **Feature creation via binning for non-numeric data:** Creating new features out of raw data is not only limited to numeric data. For example, you could classify movies according to type: action, romantic comedy, horror, and so on. Software that analyzes text can be applied to the movie review to extract a variety of classification features that denote movie type. Software that analyzes images can classify an image as cat or dog, happy or sad. For classification data, the value of the feature is binary (Y or N).

Overfitting versus Underfitting

Adding features to a data set increases the set of variables available as predictors. But adding too many features may increase the time required to train the model. And the resulting model, by aligning with every data point of the training set, may not project well to new data. Such a model follows the noise in a particular data set, but misses the pattern that holds across data sets. This is the problem of overfitting. The opposite problem of overfitting is underfitting. Underfitting occurs when a model of low complexity does not align well with the training data. The model may have been built on too few features to capture the underlying pattern in the data. For such an oversimplified model, there is a high degree of error between the value predicted by the model and the actual value in the training data.

This discussion points to two characteristics that can be used to describe predictive models. Bias is the degree to which a model oversimplifies the relationships inherent in the data. Variance is the degree to which a model follows a specific data set too closely. Overfitting is a condition wherein the model has low bias, but high variance. Underfitting is a condition wherein the model has high bias, but low variance. Models that exhibit either overfitting or underfitting are unlikely to generalize well, failing to predict values accurately when exposed to data sets outside of the training data set. The best models strike a balance between overfitting and underfitting, capturing the pattern and not the noise within the data.

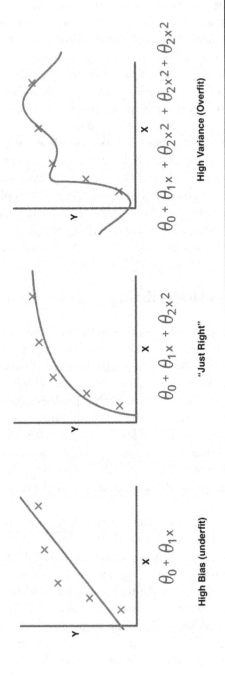

Figure 3-4 Underfitting versus Overfitting

Overfitting versus Underfitting for a Model Predicting Housing Prices

To better understand the challenges of overfitting and underfitting, it is helpful to compare the three charts in Figure 3-4. Each chart shows the same set of data points relating the price of a house (*Y*-axis) and the size of a house (*X*-axis). The model in each chart is the line drawn through the data points that expresses the relationship between house size and house price.

This chart depicts a simple model. It was built by a linear regression algorithm that yielded a straight-line function. This model assumes that as square footage goes up, price goes up in a linear fashion, that is, with a constant rate of change. A look at the chart shows that there are significant differences or errors between the model's predicted values and the actual values in the data. It is not surprising that other factors (such as location) have a big impact in determining price. We know, for example, that a smaller house in a fancy neighborhood costs much more than a larger house in a run-down neighborhood. If that's true, then the relationship between house price and house size cannot be linear. A model that relies on simplifying assumptions, missing the true relationship, is said to have high bias. The flaws in this model illustrate the problem of underfitting.

The chart on the right illustrates a model that expresses the relationship between square footage and price as a fourth-degree polynomial. This model fits the data points of the training data set the closest of the three alternatives shown. But it's hard to believe that this model with its many ups and downs can generalize well to new data. New data (not part of the training data set) would almost surely not have this detailed pattern of sudden price increases and price decreases at precisely these size points. This model is said to have high variance, with too much dependence on the details of the test data set. Variance refers to the amount by which a model would change if we trained it on a different data set. The flaws in this model illustrate the problem of overfitting.

The chart in the middle assumes that the relationship between square footage and price is a smooth curve that can be expressed by a quadratic equation. This function looks to express the overall trend in the data the best of the three alternatives. This model is likely to perform better than the other alternatives when applied to new data, which is different than the training data. It sets the right balance between bias and variance—that is, between underfitting and overfitting.

In practice, overfitting is a far more common problem than underfitting. So how can you guard against overfitting? Here are several suggestions:

- **Reduce the number of features in the data set:** Deleting features that are either redundant or unrelated to the outcome the model seeks to predict can reduce the risk of overfitting.

- **Expand the data set:** Another corrective for overfitting is to increase the size of the data set. The portion for training and the portion for testing will each be larger. To be effective, this strategy requires that the expanded data set is not only bigger but also more diversified. Recall that hiring bias, not by superior performance, caused the overrepresentation of male musicians in symphony orchestras several decades ago. Expanding the training data with similar data from other orchestras of the time would not have helped.
- **Ensemble modeling techniques:** An ensemble approach to machine learning, such as random forest, can be helpful in guarding against overfitting. Random forest is a machine learning algorithm that creates multiple decision trees. The average prediction of the individual trees is selected to be the resulting model. Basing the final model on the results of multiple modeling efforts reduces the risk of a single modeling effort following the noise in the data. This ensemble approach to machine learning has been proven to be a method that can address the related issues of overfitting and accidental correlations.

From Model Development and Deployment Back to Data Acquisition and Preparation

With a prepared data set as the foundation, a predictive model is developed using a combination of features (the input variables) to predict the target feature (the output variable). For example, a real estate model to predict market prices relies on data about a house (features such as number and type of rooms, size, location, and age) in order to predict the target feature—selling price.

For a machine learning application, the data is typically split on a ratio of 90/10 between a training data set and a test data set. The training data set is used for learning which feature or combination of features have the greatest impact on the target feature—selling price—the feature which we seek to predict. The other portion of the data is held out as a test set used to evaluate how accurately the model predicts the actual sale prices at a point in time.

The data cycle continues after model development to data acquisition and data preparation. After initial model development, additional data preparation may be required. For example, the data scientist may need to create new features or delete some existing features. In many cases, more data may need to be added. A revised model is then developed and tested. The cycle continues until the model is ready for production.

Chapter 4

Building Models to Support Augmented Intelligence

Introduction

Building models is complex because it requires that you understand the business process you are focused on. In addition, models are dynamic. It is imperative that the best machine learning (ML) algorithms are selected, tested, and refined as new data is introduced. In this chapter, we discuss the different types of machine learning algorithms and some of the ways in which they are used. We explain what it means to build a model that will support augmented intelligence.

Augmented intelligence requires models that are constantly refined to capture new data that reflects both business process and new information changes. Once you have selected and prepared your data based on the business process you are addressing, the most important next step is to build your model by selecting the machine learning algorithm that best fits the task. Creating and executing a model is neither a one-step nor a one-time process; rather it is an iterative cycle. You begin by selecting an algorithm and then run the algorithm over the majority of the data to create the model. Once the model is created, the hard work begins, since you must evaluate the model using the portion of the data that was not used to build the model. Then, when your model is in use, you must continually retest it when the data changes. Significant changes in data may require you to rebuild your model.

Explaining Machine Learning Models

A machine learning model uses mathematical techniques to create a model from a data set. Subsequently, this model can be used to address a specific business problem or challenge. The model is built by using an algorithm that can find meaningful contextual patterns in the initial data. Once the model has been trained with the appropriate data, it is used to help the organization make predictions about their business as new data comes in. If executed well, these models can help guide human experts to make well-informed decisions. Data preparation is critical to ensuring that your model is indeed predictive.

Once you identify the information, you must choose an algorithm that is appropriate for the data, which will be discussed in detail in the next section. The algorithm runs on your data and builds a model that is then used for new data that comes from your business. However, first you must evaluate the model to ascertain that it works. Evaluation is not simply a process of feeding some data into the algorithm and getting a model with the assumption that results are correct. You need to be able to test the data to assume that the results are performing well. One important approach that helps you ensure the accuracy of a model is by training with data where the results are already known. At this point, you can continue to add additional well-understood data where the results are also known. Thereafter, when the model is in use, it must be tested periodically as your business data grows. What are you testing for? You need to test for both accuracy of results and hidden biases within those data sets that will give you results that will hurt your business. Because your data and your model are not static, this type of testing and evaluation will go on forever. As your business changes and new data is introduced—such as information about new products, new customers, and changing partnerships—you will inevitably need to change your model. Typically, business changes will result in business process changes that we discussed in Chapter 3. But you cannot leave this to chance. It is important that you establish a business process that establishes a way to initiate a new cycle of data testing and model reexamination.

Understanding the Role of ML Algorithms

All machine learning algorithms are computer programs that classify a set of examples into different categories. It is important to understand the differences between the many types of algorithms and how they are best used to build your models. Despite the fact that there are more than 40 machine learning algorithms, they fall into the following two categories:

- Inspectable algorithms
- Opaque or blackbox algorithms

Inspectable Algorithms

An inspectable algorithm allows you to review the results and understand what the model is doing. Decision trees are the only algorithm that enables a user to inspect and gain insights into the results produced by the algorithm. Decision trees have existed since the 1960s and continue to be used. However, they have a major limitation: Decision trees cannot support a large number of features or large data sets. Because of these scalability limitations, it can be difficult to ascertain the patterns that are at the heart of machine learning for large data sets. Despite the fact that inspectability or explainability is instrumental in successfully understanding what models are doing, decision trees serve as only one type of tool in the machine learning predictive toolbox.

Now let's look a little closer at how decision trees work. By understanding them, you will recognize the value of a ML algorithm. Looking a little closer at how this algorithm functions, you will see that it captures relationships among categories by making decisions as it branches down the tree on what feature matters in the decision in the tree. The "leaf" or ends of the tree represent the categories.

Let's start with a hypothetical example. Suppose that a tire company wants to know the causes of tire failures at less than 6 months of age of their tires. The tire engineers must first create the data set for the algorithm to use. This process is not trivial and takes some guess work and a lot of data modeling to get the data ready to be used. The tire engineers guess that important features of the data could include the type of tire (model 01, 02, 03), the chemical types (assume these are rubber and synthetic nylon, for this discussion), the tire weight, and the length of time it was stored. Scientific articles suggest that the day of the week might also be a feature, because workers tend to be less productive and mindful on Mondays. The engineers decide to use as features for storage amounts of less than 5 days and equal to or more than 5 days. The same algorithm could be run with different time features to see what results occur. Although the discussion below uses terms such as rubber, synthetic, and days of the week, in fact those values would need to be turned into numerical forms (1 or 2 for tire type; 1–7 for days of the week, and so on) for processing in the algorithm.

The algorithm uses these features for each example in the data set it learns from. It creates the decision tree as it learns from examples in the data set provided by the company. The hypothetical resulting trees would look like the ones in Figure 4-1 on the next page.

Inspecting these results, one sees that (1) tire weight and model did not matter, as they are not factors in the decision trees; (2) overall rubber tires had higher failure rates than synthetics; and (3) storage and creation on Monday for both categories of tires were a problem but worse for rubber. The highest

If Tire Type is Rubber

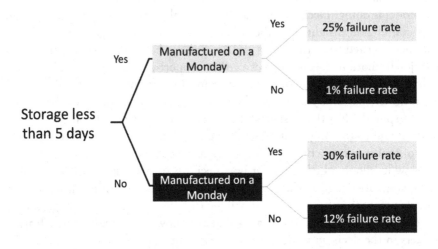

If Tire Type is Synthetic Nylon

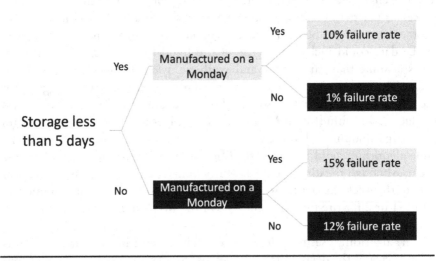

Figure 4-1   Decision Trees for Tire Failures

failure rates were for rubber tires stored more than 5 days and created on a Monday. There is no guarantee that using a larger data set with the same features would result in the same tree, but unless the smaller data set is anomalous in its examples, the larger data set might have slightly different results but not be fundamentally different. Checking that assumption is very important in using machine learning algorithms as well as trying different features of the tires. This decision tree tells the engineers what kind of failure rates they can expect for their tires depending on when they were made. However, over time, if the engineers improve their tire manufacturing, a new data set might show different results from the one in this example. So it is critical to keep collecting new data and seeing what results occur for that data.

Note that, importantly, decision tree algorithms are not widely used when there are a large number of features or when the data set is quite large because the algorithm runs too slowly to produce the model. So why use decision trees at all? In inspecting the decision tree, developers and business users can explain just how it is that a new tire will be categorized. Imagine if the tree was not inspectable. We would place a black piece of paper on the whole tree in the diagram and just leave the bottom leaves of the tree to look at. Then, when a given tire was run through the model, the results would simply show that it had one of the failure rates at the leaves of the tree. No one would know why that tire had that failure rate, or what features contribute to that failure rate, and they could not use the algorithm to decide what to change in their business process! Obviously knowing the predicted failure rate is useful, but knowing why is even more so. Furthermore, inspecting the tree may also help the human team see if there is bias in the original data, a matter we will elaborate upon in Chapter 5.

Black Box Algorithms

The vast majority of machine learning algorithms provide non-inspectable results. The algorithms are often called black box algorithms because unlike a decision tree, you can't look inside to see how the algorithm works. Non-inspection means that the way that the algorithm makes its choices is not something that a data scientist or anyone else can look at, just like when we put black paper over the decision tree. As a result, black box algorithms require other methods to see whether they are producing reasonable results.

Opaque or black box algorithms do not provide the analyst with an understanding of why the algorithm produced its results. The algorithm makes choices and reaches conclusions based on how it interprets the data. Therefore, if an organization needs to explain how a conclusion was arrived at, it will require different methods to explain the results. For example, if a machine learning algorithm is used to make hiring recommendations, an organization may be required to explain why certain individuals were hired and why others were not considered.

There are two types of opaque algorithms: supervised and unsupervised. As we discussed in Chapter 2, a supervised model is one in which you begin with an established set of data that is already classified. This classified data has labeled features that define the meaning of the data. In contrast, unsupervised models are based on a large volume of unlabeled data that must be classified based on a pattern or cluster.

Supervised Algorithms

All supervised algorithms start with examples for which the data scientist knows how the classification should go (sometimes called the gold standard). The algorithm must learn this classification. However, because the rules the algorithm learns cannot be inspected, some of the examples must be set aside for later evaluation (called the test set or test data). The standard protocol for these algorithms is to have the algorithm train on the majority of the examples, called the training set or training data, which is often 90% of the examples. The remaining 10% of the data are the test set. The algorithm is never trained using the test set because it would eliminate the method of seeing how the algorithm performs on "new" data. When the algorithm finishes on the training set, it is then evaluated by testing it using a test set to see how well it performs.

Creating a Gold Standard for Supervised Learning

It is not enough to simply classify data. Ensuring the accuracy of models requires that subject matter experts understand the data being used to feed the model. Achieving accuracy requires a process that produces trust in the data and its model. Creating a gold standard for classification is one of the most predicable techniques. Gold standards allow the expert to guarantee that results are accurate. For example, a human can quickly ascertain that a human face is either a man, woman, or child. However, who the individual is in that picture is much more difficult; human experts can be wrong. So sometimes one needs three experts to make choices, after which their choices are compared to come up with a best-of-three decision. As a result, creating a gold standard may take a lot of time, human labor, and know how. Consider the tire example again. Data scientists and engineers must go through all of the tires in the data set and note which ones failed before and after 6 months. If the data team is missing information on failures or when the tires were made, the data can be "made up" using averages from the whole data set (although doing so may introduce errors that will show up when testing is done).

Once the data set is created, it must be divided in a random way to keep 10% for testing. Of course, there is always the chance that what appears in the test set is different in some way from the training set. If that happens, there will be a pattern that the model has not seen and will misinterpret. It is just such cases that testing is meant to check for. Simply said, the data team wants to know how well the model works on this test set. Another way to test the data is to choose the training and test sets 10 different times (called 10-fold cross validation). The algorithm is trained and tested on each group and then compared to see on average how well the tests performed.

Usually ML algorithms do not perform perfectly on test data sets, but performance above 85% is often taken as reliable. That percentage may not be reliable enough, and can be resolved by company managers making judgments based on such matters as the cost of errors. A business might be quite right to ask for performance above 95%. For example, returning to the tire failure scenario, suppose the learning algorithm predicts only 85% of the failures, which means it fails to predict 15% of the tire failures. If those failures cost the company significant time and money to replace (as well as affecting the company's reputation), the learning algorithm may not be used. The data team will need to try again, by requiring additional features that were not previously considered or more data examples that provide more information and may lead to better performance.

How does augmented intelligence play a role in data testing? Simply said, testing does not happen only once. Over time, your business may change, and the data will reflect that change. The model used for the data will need to be retrained and retested to assume that it is still making good predictions. The team who works with the model will need to do periodic remodeling to see if the new model makes different predictions based on the combination of new and old data. Conclusion: You can't just introduce a machine learning model into your business process and expect it to perform perfectly forever. You need human team members to "keep an eye" on the algorithm and make sure it still works well.

There are two supervised learning algorithms that are most often used in model building—k-nearest neighbors (k-NN) and support vector machines (SVM). K-nearest neighbors is the simplest and most often used type of classification algorithm. Support vector machines are used to analyze data for classification and regression analysis.

K-Nearest Neighbors

K-nearest neighbors works by taking an example's value and then locating another example value that is close to it (thus the term nearest neighbor). What counts as close in distance depends on the particular features that the data scientist chooses. For the tire example, these features could be age (in whole numbers of 1 to 120), weight (in whole numbers or real numbers), and so on. This algorithm can create many clusters (not just failure or no failure for the tire business).

An important challenge for this algorithm is the size of k. The k in a k-NN algorithm stands for a number that is a positive integer that must be chosen when running the algorithm. If k is too small, the algorithm will overfit the data, which means it will fail to predict certain members of the clusters. Splitting into a training and test set, and keeping the test set large enough, helps to reduce overfitting. If k is too large, irrelevant examples will creep into clusters and make the algorithm unreliable. Irrelevant examples are referred to as outliers. Data scientists sometimes have ways of visualizing data (with graphs) that allow them to remove outliers from the data set before the algorithm works, but data sets with many features do not make this visualization straightforward. So data experts often try several different values of k in order to see how well the algorithm performs on the training set and the test set. Of course, test sets are never used for training data.

Support Vector Machines

A support vector machine is widely used when there are a small number of features to train on, where "small" depends on the number of features relative to the number of items in the data set. The tire example discussed so far has a much smaller number of features relative to the typical data set in most companies. A support vector machine makes its decisions not by simply drawing a line between the members of the data set. Instead, it chooses a margin around that line and looks to make the margin as wide as possible.

There are many kinds of support vector machine algorithms, which grow in complexity with the mathematics that govern them (from linear SVMs to ones with quadratic functions and beyond). Most data scientists prefer linear SVMs or ones that use quadratics because they are simpler to compute. SVMs have been used to classify texts (to determine which of a set of prespecified categories a text most closely fits), perform facial recognition (to find the face or faces in an image), image classification (again to pick the prespecified category in which the image fits), interpret handwritten letters, and to classify proteins. Note that in all of these applications, a set of classes is prespecified, not invented by the algorithm. Like other supervised machine learning algorithms, SVMs rely on people to provide the shape of the problem that the machine algorithm is to learn, and the algorithm provides the (non-inspectable) rules to predict which category an example will fit into.

Here we take a moment to consider a business problem application so that we can understand how algorithms might work with it. A cable television company that provides video content to viewers wants to know what advertisements to show to its customer viewers while they watch a show or movie. The data that the company has will include customer location, the show being watched, the history of other shows watched, the time of day (morning, afternoon, early evening, late evening, past-midnight), and the content package the customer pays for (for example, bare bones, many channels, special channels, etc.). The company may purchase information about the income level of the customer (such data is readily available), but it may still not have certain types of significant data, such as the gender and age of the viewer, and whether a group or a single individual is watching. This missing data might be crucial to the model and is a potential weakness in the model.

The company must determine what categories of advertisements it wants the algorithm to display using the data set and the categories of location, show, and so on. For example, does the company have six different categories of advertisements it wants to consider or does it not know what categories of advertisements it should use? When the company knows the categories of advertisements it wants to categorize its data into, it can choose a supervised algorithm. The algorithm will create a model that has learned a way to decide the categories of advertisements to show viewers as they watch a particular show. For example, the model might have learned that evening viewers watching shows about international travel should be shown advertisements about cars and household appliances. However, the cable company must also assure that both training and test sets contain representative data for each of the categories that the algorithm will learn from or else the learned model will make poor predictions for some viewers. If the company does not have a way to create such sets, it is best to turn to unsupervised algorithms. Furthermore, if the company does not know what categories it wants, it can use unsupervised algorithms to determine the categories and put values into each.

Unsupervised Algorithms

Unsupervised learning algorithms for clustering tasks fall into two broad classes: K-means clustering and hierarchical clustering. There are other types of tasks for unsupervised learning to reduce the dimensionality of a problem, but such tasks are often used by data scientists in order to simplify problems. K-means clustering is one of the simplest and commonly used unsupervised machine learning algorithms. The objective of K-means is to group similar data points in order to visually discover underlying patterns. K-means clustering starts by picking k centroids (the points around which each cluster will eventually form) and interactively finds points close to each cluster, moving the centroid as needed so that the centroid remains the average point for the cluster.

Hierarchical clustering also creates clusters/categories that have a hierarchical structure. In this case, the top of the hierarchy comprises the most general categories, and the subclusters have more specific categories. Hierarchical clusters begin with a number of clusters and proceed to merge them based on the proximity of cluster members to each other. Which of these two clustering techniques are to be chosen depends on the type of result the data scientist wants for the problem at hand. If you are trying to determine the best ads to display to a user of an online site with a general category such as clothing or furniture, then k-means clustering will be chosen. But if the company wants to have more specific categories as well as general ones (i.e., furniture and kitchen tables), then hierarchical clustering will be useful.

How are unsupervised algorithms evaluated for accuracy? Generally, creating a gold standard corpus is too labor intensive. For clustering techniques, one can measure how close each piece of data is to other pieces of data in the cluster and how far the centroids of each cluster are to other clusters. A number of other very mathematically sophisticated techniques have been explored by data scientists and will not be explained here.

Since all black box algorithms are non-inspectable, must it always be the case that you can't learn how they work? There is considerable ongoing research to determine scalable and predictable ways to inspect black box algorithms. However, thus far no single approach has emerged as the solution to the interpretability or explainability of models.

Understanding Reinforcement Learning and Neural Networks

There are some important algorithms that function like a combination of supervised and unsupervised models. The most important of these are reinforcement learning and neural networks. Reinforcement learning is a model that receives feedback on its performance to guide it to a good outcome. The system learns based on trial and error. Neural networks are designed to emulate human brains. These networks consist of input nodes, hidden layers, and output nodes. Neural networks are being used in recommendation engines and speech recognition.

Reinforcement learning (RL) has only recently been used in business applications because the way it learns is not so easily adapted to business problems. In RL, the algorithm experiences positive and negative rewards as it makes choices and develops rules inside the model (its choices are called policies). Suppose that the algorithm is playing a simulated game of soccer, where it can kick the ball to another team player, try to kick a goal, or try to steal the ball from an opponent.

It chooses an action based on features of the environment (which it chooses for itself) and then takes one of the three actions. If it fails, it gets a negative reward; if it succeeds, it gets a positive reward. It updates the reasons (the policies) for its choices based on the rewards and keeps going. Clearly, game-playing programs benefit from using RL, but other recent business applications have started to appear. For example, suppose our cable television company uses its unsupervised algorithm to decide which types of advertisements to show its customers and now it must bid on ads from several different companies that create ads. An RL model could decide on the basis of the cost of ads, length of ads, and whatever else it determines relevant to which ad to bid on. Then its reward is whether the customer watches the ad (positive reward), turns off the sound (negative reward), or turns off the show (negative reward). Based on those positive and negative rewards, it adjusts its policies for the next ad choices.

Neural network algorithms include so called "deep" neural network algorithms. These algorithms consist of a set of calculations done on "nodes," each of which is linked to other nodes. In simple neural nets, there are a layer of input nodes, one middle layer of nodes (called the hidden layer), and one layer of output nodes. Figure 4-2 shows connections between the top nodes of the network and all the other nodes. Although a typical network only has three rows of nodes, it is possible to add many more.

This complex network was designed to work something like the neurons in the human brain, though these artificial neural networks are vastly simpler than human neurons and their networks.

The mathematics of neural network algorithms works in the following way. Each node has weights for each input value of that node and a summation function for all the weights. Each summation function has an activation function that determines what output will be provided for that node and its various inputs. Thus, every node in the network has summation and activation functions all

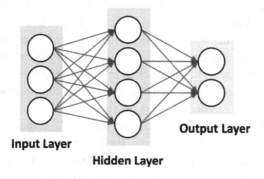

Figure 4-2 Neural Network Composed of Three Layers

making guesses at the correct answer and then adjusting the weights to reduce the error when the node guesses incorrectly.

The neural network is designed to optimize the weights to reduce the error in a correct output. Simple neural networks were, for much of their history, used as supervised learning algorithms, and so the outputs were known for each input. Much of the research in machine learning has explored a wide range of optimization algorithms and activation functions, which will not be discussed in this chapter. In addition, several more specialized types of neural networks have been invented, including feedforward and self-organizing map neural networks, to name just a few. Neural networks have been used for classification problems and clustering (the similarities of some set). Unsupervised simple neural networks have been used to recognize faces, perform speech recognition, make predictions for cancer diagnosis, and for long-term financial forecasting, to name a few examples.

American Express was one of the first companies in the 1990s to use machine learning algorithms to detect fraud in credit card use. American Express evolved their credit and fraud risk management practice from a manual process based on training individuals into a data- and science-based organization.[1] The American Express project was intended to identify patterns of fraud in credit card transactions. The results proved that machine learning models could in fact identify fraud. The value came from American Express's ability to feed the system with massive amounts of the right data. By detecting patterns that would result in fraud, American Express saved an enormous amount of money. To this day, American Express has continued to heavily invest in machine learning technologies and has industry-leading credit and fraud write-off rates. The success of the project was one of the early indications that machine learning and pattern-based algorithms could become an engine for business transformation. In addition to preventing fraud, American Express was able to offer credit to a broader range of individuals.

Currently, neural network algorithms have been devised to detect credit card fraud in real-time. However, such detection continues to be an active area of work for credit card companies who naturally do not share their algorithms publicly.

In recent years, attention has shifted to deep neural networks and the associated notion of deep learning. Rather than one hidden layer, deep neural networks have many hidden layers, only limited by the compute power to manage the computations. In essence, there is no theoretical way to define the correct number of layers for a given problem. The idea of these many layers is to have each layer train on a given feature and then pass its results to the next layer, which trains on another feature. Deep neural networks are put forward as dealing with highly complex data and finding structure in that data without supervision. Both simple and deep neural network algorithms require substantial data to do their decision making, and for deep neural networks, the amount of data needed is immense. In addition, the amount of computation for large simple neural nets and for any deep neural net can be extensive, so data and computation are major factors in using these kinds of learning algorithms.

The Value of Machine Learning Models

There are a variety of machine learning algorithms that are incredibly useful in helping organizations gain insights and value from their data and business processes. Applying the right type of algorithms can create models that are able to provide the right type of insights and context for the data. However, you need to recognize that a model in isolation can be risky since you cannot assume that you will be able to have 100% accuracy. Therefore, it is imperative that you include subject matter experts in your model-design process. One of the most effective uses of models for complex business decision making is to use them in collaboration with human experts.

Summary

In this chapter, we have discussed the process of building a model for a business problem from a machine learning algorithm running over well-prepared data. We have explored several types of machine learning algorithms—inspectable ones, especially decision trees, and black box ones, including supervised and nonsupervised algorithms, reinforcement learning, and neural networks. We have discussed the need for evaluating the data with training and testing sets for supervised algorithms and methods for evaluating nonsupervised algorithms. We have also discussed how augmentation occurs, that is, how business teams—both the data team and the team working with the algorithm every day—play a role in managing the data, the algorithm, and the model over time for business decisions.

Chapter 5

Augmented Intelligence in a Business Process

Introduction

Humans and machines working in collaboration can have a powerful impact on the effectiveness of business processes. Augmented intelligence overcomes the limitations of isolating human understanding from the massive amounts of both structured and unstructured data available to analyze complexity in record time. So, how does augmented intelligence change business processes and the way that work is getting done?

Defining the Business Process in Context with Augmented Intelligence

A business process represents a series of tasks that are performed in a prescribed end-to-end sequence. There are two techniques for applying augmented intelligence to improve an end-to-end business process: weak augmentation or strong augmentation. In addition, there are situations in which organizations will need a combination of weak and strong augmentation. Let's look at what each of these business process approaches consists of.

Weak Augmentation

There are many situations in which automation is undertaken to streamline a set of repetitive business processes. For example, a worker may be required to insert the same information multiple times in a series of forms that are part of a single business process. This could be a newly insured motorist who is buying a policy and needs to have the same data in a series of related forms. Often, there are business processes that require that the worker understand precisely which forms are needed in which sequence to execute in a business process. One of the benefits of weak augmentation is that it is fast to implement because the processes themselves are not changing. Therefore, this is a pragmatic approach to saving time and money through straightforward process automation. The automation does require some level of intelligence, since the machine needs to be able to understand the patterns of the text fields being automated. Automating the ability to place the correct information in the right place solves a time problem but does not address the efficiency of the process itself.

Understanding Weak Augmentation

In weak augmentation, the flow of tasks from beginning to end is unchanged. However, machine labor is substituted for human labor for the more routine tasks within the process flow, where machines have an advantage in terms of speed and accuracy. For example, a process might require a series of forms to be manually filled in by clerical staff, even though the same data is filled in over and over again as you move from form to form. This task, manually performed, is inefficient, prone to error, and costly to apply. Augmented intelligence can be deployed to map differently named fields across separate forms—each field capturing the same data. Once this mapping has been established, the fields can be manually filled in once and then the data can be automatically applied (following the map) to fill in the same fields on related forms.

Weak augmentation is the low-hanging fruit of business process improvement. The automation of the form-filling task by an application of augmented intelligence results in increased productivity and efficiency through a process now executed by a mix of human and machine labor. This approach of automating steps of an existing business process is sometimes termed "lift and shift" in that a process is lifted from its former environment (human labor only) to a new environment (a mix of human and machine labor). The term "lift and shift" is borrowed from the world of outsourcing, where a services company is hired by a company to perform a specific process, following the same steps as before, but shifting it to a geography where labor is cheaper. The shift occurs without any changes to the sequence of tasks in the work process.

Not surprisingly, outsourcing services companies are now revising their business model to incorporate augmented intelligence for cost-saving advantages. Instead of relying on finding the cheapest labor markets to get tasks done manually for less cost, they are investing in AI for greater and more sustainable cost advantages. The new "lift and shift" occurs when the services company substitutes machine performance of tasks for human performance of tasks. This automation approach is proving to be a more efficient way to deliver outsourcing services on behalf of their clients.

Invoice Processing as Weak Augmentation

Consider a traditional invoicing process. It comprises a series of well-defined steps:

1. A purchase order is issued by a company (the buyer) and sent to a vendor (the seller) as a specification of a request to buy goods.
2. A report of goods received records the event when goods shipped by the vendor arrive at the company.
3. An invoice is issued by the vendor requesting payment for the goods received.
4. The three documents are matched to ensure that the invoice is accurate, that it is not a duplicate, and that the invoice corresponds to the goods that were requested and then received.
5. Once the three-way match is verified, the invoice is entered into the accounts payable (AP) module of the financial system. Then, it can be scheduled for payment.
6. The invoice is paid according to the schedule, with payment sent from the company to the vendor.
7. The AP module is updated by debiting the appropriate payables account to reflect the event, marking payment to the vendor.

Since this is a routine process, with applicable rules governing each step (or task), there is a good potential for automation. Step 4, for example, requires the matching up of fields from three different documents. To facilitate the matching, a mapping table must be built (and then maintained) to link up fields from each document that capture the same data. Once the mapping table is established, the three documents can be matched up in an automated fashion. Then, in Step 5, the mapping is extended to a fourth document—a form within the accounts payable system.

Each of the tasks that consult the mapping table (i.e., in Steps 4 and 5) can be done in a machine-automated way via robotic process automation (RPA). RPA is a set of tools based on bots (automated-process libraries). These tools differ from traditional automation interactions because they include features that allow data to be handled across multiple applications. This automation follows the field-matching rules embedded in the mapping table.

RPA as Weak Augmentation

Robotic process automation is a technique that has gained considerable traction over the past few years because of its ability to quickly automate repetitive office tasks. This is in contrast to traditional manufacturing automation that focuses on taking one portion of a workflow or even just one task and creating a robot to specialize in it. Office work often requires the same types of repetition, but it is data being manipulated across platforms and applications, so a physical robot is not necessary. Instead, a software robot is deployed with the ability to launch and operate other software.

Robotic process automation and artificial intelligence (AI) each represent a means to provide a level of automation of a task, or even the entire sequence of tasks within a business process, by following a set of rules. For certain steps within a well-defined process such as invoice handling, the rule-based approach works well. You can even specify rules to flag an exception when certain conditions are met, triggering a message to a human agent requesting a resolution of an issue before payment is approved.

Artificial intelligence capabilities can be used to extend RPA's capabilities.

- Natural language processing can be applied to understand text inside of the invoice. This capability enables detecting similarities in field names across documents.
- Machine learning can be applied to examine the data captured in each field, looking for similar patterns in data values. When two fields in separate documents have the same pattern of data values collected, this provides strong evidence that these fields can be mapped together, as they are capturing the same information.

Applying natural language processing and machine learning on top of RPA is a bridge to the enhanced form of augmented intelligence—strong augmentation.

Strong Augmentation

Strong augmentation is needed when the existing business processes are no longer enough to differentiate how a company conducts business. In strong augmentation, a business wants to be able to change business processes based on the outcomes of sophisticated predictive analytics. The more complex and sophisticated the data is, the more important it is to provide human knowledge workers with the context they need to make well-informed decisions. Some tasks that are straightforward can be done with machine automation. However, other situations will provide the knowledge worker with a variety of choices.

At this time, the knowledge worker looks at the options, which may include the percentage certainty that the option is well suited to solve the problem. In other situations, the selection is not as clear-cut. This requires that the expert examine the underlying analysis of recommended next steps. Strong augmentation is intended to provide guidance—not to simply automate a process. Why? Simply put, a professional with deep knowledge will lack the ability to ingest all the complex data in a field of study. Therefore, to have access to data to support decision making can make the difference between success and failure. Strong augmentation helps a business to redesign an entire process via a new mix of tasks that gets the work done in a new way via machine–human collaboration. For example, rather than simply automating manual processes, strong augmentation applies machine learning techniques to help humans reimage a complex business process in new and innovative ways. This would not be possible to achieve with machine learning alone or human experts in isolation.

Strong Augmentation: Business Process Redesign

In strong augmentation, the process flow is changed to better leverage the synergies of human–machine collaboration. By taking advantage of machine learning and natural language processing, the techniques that can be used to get better results can improve process execution.

To redesign a business process, you need to understand the current business process and have insight on how machine intelligence could be applied to improve the process. Hybrid professionals have the benefit of being able to combine a business process and intelligent technology expertise. These professionals are in the best position to recommend business process changes that can exploit the potential of augmented intelligence.

To understand strong augmentation within a redesigned business process, let's examine two processes in the operations of the MoneyMaker Mining Company that have been changed through the use of augmented intelligence. The first process is predictive maintenance, and the second is predictive sourcing.

Though the company is fictitious, the examples reflect the actual experience of companies that are deploying augmented intelligence to change the way work gets done and to achieve better outcomes than were possible before. In each case, the process has been rethought so as to enable human–machine collaboration.

Strong Augmentation for Predictive Maintenance

You work in the maintenance department of MoneyMaker Mining Company, responsible for the maintenance of the heavy equipment required to drill for valuable minerals in the mines. The company is headquartered in Santiago, the capital of Chile, while the drilling operations are over 1000 miles to the north near the Bolivian border. When a critical piece of heavy equipment fails, output is reduced until the equipment is repaired. If parts are not available locally, it can take days to get the needed parts, and the missed output is costly for the company. It is a key priority for MoneyMaker to improve the equipment-maintenance process. They commit to invest in predictive-maintenance applications so that they can get advance warning of impending equipment failures. This example illustrates the intersection of process, technology, and people that is a hallmark of augmented intelligence.

A new business process for equipment maintenance was established to provide assistance to the maintenance people in the field and the planners at company headquarters. The new process, built on machine intelligence, is composed of the following steps:

1. **Data Acquisition:** An array of sensors collects data from a range of parts in the equipment over a period of time.
2. **Data Exploration:** Analytical methods, including machine learning, mine the sensor data looking for patterns, searching for signals that indicate a likely future equipment failure.
3. **Prediction:** The pattern is expressed as a prediction, such as, "When sensor reading x is observed, failure of equipment due to issue y is likely within the next 2 weeks."
4. **Recommendation:** The prediction is associated with a recommendation for action to be taken by the human maintenance specialist close to field operations. For example, the recommendation could state: "Change part within the next three weeks to avoid equipment failure due to an electrical short circuit." The recommendation could also trigger a request to ship the needed part to the remote field operation.
5. **Monitoring:** Data coming from the equipment's sensors is monitored on an ongoing basis, looking for signals of imminent failures. When this condition is encountered, the recommended action is communicated to the maintenance specialist.
6. **Action:** The field maintenance specialist (working at the drilling operations site) approves the order to ship out the part (per the recommendation) and replaces the part when it is received within the timeframe indicated.
7. **Monitoring:** Through a combination of machine collection and analysis of sensor data with human oversight, the status of the equipment is monitored to ensure that the fix was successful.

A related process (equipment-maintenance scheduling and planning) is the responsibility of the maintenance planner at company headquarters.

Aggregating data from the operation of the equipment provides feedback on the current maintenance plan and schedule. Based on an analysis of this information, the maintenance schedule can be adjusted within the limits contained in the associated financial plan. The goal is to maximize the impact of scheduled repairs to address the most likely causes of equipment failure.

The entire maintenance cycle, from pattern discovery to planning coordinates activities, is performed by a combination of humans (maintenance specialists and maintenance planners) and intelligent machines. From the perspective of the maintenance specialists and maintenance planners, the revised business process changes the mix of tasks they are assigned. To realize the benefits in the maintenance operation, field maintenance workers and headquarters-based planners must acquire new skills to be able to interact effectively with machine intelligence and implement the machine-generated recommendations.

Strong Augmentation for Predictive Sourcing

You work in the procurement department for MoneyMaker Mining Company at headquarters in Santiago, Chile. Your company participates in a business-to-business trading network (SAP Ariba is one such business-to-business network), which brings together suppliers of goods (i.e., sellers) with consumers of goods (i.e., buyers). You are a specialist with expertise in certain types of heavy equipment required for the mining operations.

The current process works in the following way. When a request comes into procurement from the field-operations group, it is routed to the appropriate specialist. The specialist then researches the request to find a supplier, using one of the following methods:

- Search on the network and select the supplier with the equipment in hand, the lowest price, and the earliest delivery date.
- Send an email to other specialists to see if any of them have experience with the supplier you found on the network. Also, check out reports from the field, looking for any reported issues on the quality of the equipment produced by the supplier and the timeliness of their delivery.
- Check out reviews of the suppliers you are considering and select the supplier with the highest overall score.

Each of these research strategies can yield data that is relevant to your decision. But such an elaborate process can be excessive, especially when sourcing items that are reliably available from a large number of suppliers. And when sourcing routine, easily available items, this level of effort may not be necessary.

Procurement specialists can redesign this process to reflect differential treatment for a more critical versus a less critical purchasing request. The new process uses machine intelligence to assess the incoming request based on the supply risk (many or small number of qualified suppliers) and financial risk (how critical is this purchase request to a company's profitability). Sourcing paper clips is routine (with low cost and many suppliers) and, therefore, a good candidate for machine-led automation, whereas sourcing a critical piece of equipment (with high cost and few suppliers) is not. These two dimensions of purchasing risk—financial risk and supplier risk—were first developed by Peter Kraljic in 1983.[1]

Combining these principles with the capabilities of machine intelligence, the purchasing process could be redesigned as follows:

- **Low supply risk, low financial risk:** When the purchasing request, as evaluated by machine intelligence, is not critical (both supply and financial risk are low), a purchasing request is considered routine. This request can then be processed autonomously by a machine without the intervention of skilled procurement professionals.
- **High supply risk and/or high financial risk:** When the purchasing request, as evaluated by machine intelligence, is more critical (high supplier and/or financial risk), an approach that combines human and machine intelligence is needed. Machine intelligence builds a prediction by scoring capable suppliers, then delivers a recommendation to the procurement specialist who decides how to source the needed goods or services.

In building a score to evaluate candidate suppliers, the algorithm selects those factors that have been demonstrated to be most impactful in predicting a supplier's future performance. The data sources for these factors include transactions in the network, text reviews of supplier performance, and reports within your company on the performance of candidate suppliers for the needed equipment. The scoring algorithm uses methods such as machine learning, predictive analytics, and natural language processing.

Automating a subset of the tasks performed by a procurement specialist does not replace all of the skills, tasks, and responsibilities of the job. But the availability of machine intelligence changes the job, enabling specialists to concentrate on the tasks that humans are better suited to perform than machines. In the redesigned procurement process, the procurement specialist will have time to refocus on critical sourcing tasks that benefit from the human touch.

One key task is maintaining relationships with key suppliers who are the sole or nearly sole sources of critical equipment. Another task is reviewing the terms of a written contract. For contract review, there are now intelligent programs that use natural language processing to read each clause of a contract, understanding the terms and conditions expressed by this language. Routine terms and conditions can be automatically approved. But if issues are discovered, they can be flagged. The review of these exceptions then becomes the responsibility of the human procurement specialist.

We've considered two examples of augmented intelligence in a business process—predictive maintenance and predictive sourcing. *Predictive maintenance* is a process within business operations—a process that enables a business to produce or deliver its products or services. *Predictive sourcing* is another process within business operations. But sourcing is closely linked to accounts payable, one of the group of processes within financials—processes involving monetary transactions and planning. The third major process area for an organization comprises processes related to people. Predictions concerning people have unique characteristics that we will examine next.

Augmented Intelligence in a Business Process about People

What distinguishes the application of augmented intelligence in people-centered processes is that these predictions are psychologically predictive. This type of prediction takes into account data reflecting past human behavior under specific conditions and seeks to predict future human behavior under similar conditions. Where would psychologically predictive insights be useful? Marketing is a critical process area that is being fundamentally changed by machine-based predictions.

Strong Augmentation for Predictive Digital Marketing Campaign Management

Traditionally, retailers used direct mail campaigns seasonally, to either target all of their customers, or major customer segments. There were often fall, winter, spring, and summer sales, occurring on predefined calendar dates each year. The mailings went out to the list of existing customers who had already done business with the company. Sometimes the customer list was expanded by purchasing additional lists from data brokers and then sending the campaign materials to these people as well. The process of delivering the content to a customer list or lists was fairly routine, with many opportunities to automate select steps via robotic process automation.

But the move to digital marketing has dramatically changed the process of marketing campaign management. Retailers now can target individual customers (not just segments or groups of customers). Personalized content can be delivered directly to an individual customer's online environment in the context of their real-time online activities. But what content should be delivered at what time to which person? When marketing professionals create and deliver personalized content, they need to be supported by psychologically predictive algorithms that are operating at the level of an individual customer.

A predictive digital marketing campaign management process:

- uses data collected on an individual's shopping and buying habits, combined with data on where the individual lives and who he or she associates with;
- anticipates how individuals will respond to specific stimuli such as targeted online messages;
- guides the development of content and the testing of the effectiveness of that content by creative marketing professionals; and
- drives the rules for automated delivery of content to customers based on their demographic and psychological profile.

A predictive digital marketing campaign management process requires human–machine collaboration. The scale required to deliver personalized communication utilizes machine-based psychological predictions and automation. But the creative concepts behind the campaign require human involvement. Humans must not only create, but also test, monitor, and review the campaign to ensure that the results meet campaign goals.

Humans also have the responsibility to govern the process. The data privacy rights of individuals must be respected. A general opt-in for any and all uses of personal data will not comply with the European Union's influential General Data Protection Regulation (GDPR) standard. Marketers must ensure that the proper permissions are granted by the consumer covering specific actions to be taken based on the use of their personal data.

The requirement for obtaining permissions in advance severely curtails the practice of purchasing lists of additional individuals to target. After all, if you have no pre-existing relationship with a customer, you would not have had the opportunity to obtain permission to direct your content to these individuals. Achieving sufficient levels of governance is essential for determining which traditional marketing practices can be retained or need to be revised in light of the new data-driven approaches to marketing campaign management.

Redefining Fashion Retailer Business Models with Augmented Intelligence

We've considered how augmented intelligence can improve the efficiency of business processes. Applying weak augmentation, routine tasks within a process can be automated via robotic process automation. Applying strong augmentation, business process steps are redefined to take advantage of machine intelligence with algorithmic predictions and natural language processing.

But we are only at the early stages of leveraging the full impact of augmented intelligence in supporting business goals. In an era of business disruption, where new competitors are emerging to challenge market leaders, core business models are changing dramatically. Let's examine two companies in the fashion retail business that approached business-process transformation in different ways. Both The Gap, Inc., and Stitch Fix have incorporated machine-generated predictions of fashion trends in the delivery of goods and services to their customers via human–machine collaboration. These changes reflect two different business models and two different views on what humans do best and what machines do best.

Business Model Changes at The Gap, Inc., Using Algorithmic Fashion Predictions

The creative director in a fashion retailer has the task of deciding on the direction of the product lines for the future. What styles will catch on with consumers? How can forward-looking design get attention in a crowded marketplace? Fashion directors must combine experience in past trends with future insight. Historically, great designers were able to attract a following among buyers by anticipating their changing taste based on their own creativity and ability to set trends. For a fashion retailer, the creative director's decisions cascade down to multiple teams, who are responsible for bringing the fashion line to market.

With the growing use of machine-generated predictions, it wasn't long before this technology began to be applied to the realm of fashion. The challenge in applying machine intelligence to anticipate and predict fashion trends can change suddenly. So training a predictive model using last year's data may not yield a great prediction for next year's fashions.

The Gap, Inc., is a long-time fashion retailer, founded in 1969, which had seen declining sales in recent years, especially for the marquee Gap brand. The company also owns Banana Republic and, until recently, Old Navy. In response to the sales downturn, Art Peck, the CEO of The Gap, Inc., decided in 2016 to dismiss the creative directors at each of the company's brands. He told *The Wall Street Journal* that creative directors were "false messiahs," implying that their predictions were not a reliable guide to fashion trends and to critical merchandising decisions for the chain's stores.[2] In place of the creative directors, Peck brought in a data science team to develop algorithms to predict fashion trends, setting the direction for designers and merchandisers at the company.[3] At the same time, Peck instituted a process to ensure that the supply chain suppliers (moving manufacturing from Asia to the Caribbean) would be able to get products to market faster, given the volatility of fashion tastes by consumers.

The switch from relying on humans (creative directors) to relying on machines (algorithms) to predict fashion trends was part of a major business model change for the company. Moreover, relying on machine prediction rather than human prediction represents a radically different view on what machines do best and what humans do best. This reliance on machine-based prediction led to a rethinking of how humans and machines collaborate at the firm.

Have the business model changes been effective? Since the time of the CEO's decision, the Gap brand has had declining year over year sales for nearly every quarter. Of the major brands, Old Navy has achieved the best results. Finally, a decision was made in February 2019 to divide the company into two pieces, separating the Old Navy brand from the other brands of the company (the largest being the Gap and Banana Republic).[4] It is not yet clear about what further adjustments to the business model for the Gap and for the new company will be made as each seeks to optimize the mix of machine versus human labor in the production and delivery of clothing fashions.

Another Fashion Retailing Business Model Using Algorithmic Predictions: Stitch Fix

Stitch Fix is a fashion retailer that was founded in 2011 and went public in 2017. Like the Gap, it combines algorithms with human judgment in the delivery of clothing to customers on a subscription basis. Stitch Fix had a very different business model from the Gap. There are no retail stores. Instead, customers subscribe to a service in which they receive five items of clothing in a box shipped to their home on a periodic basis. The customer selects which clothes to keep and which to send back.

Algorithmic predictions drive recommendations of what clothing to send to a customer in their box, initially based on a survey that each customer fills out when they begin a relationship with Stitch Fix. As a customer begins to make selections to purchase from their subscription, the data on sales is captured and used to tune future predictions that drive future selections on merchandise for the customer's box. There is also an integration with Pinterest, where customers can post their clothing collections. This provides an additional source of personal data for developing future versions of the algorithm, tuning the prediction to reflect the tastes of individual customers.

There are two key roles in the process:

- Data scientists build and maintain the predictive algorithms that drive recommendations on what clothing to send to each customer.

- Personal stylists combine the insight gained from the algorithmic prediction with their own knowledge of the customer to guide the merchandise selection for the box. The stylists then continue to engage with customers to build business and aid retention.

As reported in 2018, Stitch Fix employed 75 data scientists and 3,000 personal stylists.[5]

The redesigned process features strong augmentation for the successful execution of the process. The model for human–machine collaboration at Stitch Fix (algorithm–stylist–customer) is a redesign of the merchandising process from that at a traditional retailer. The unique Stitch Fix method of delivering a personalized collection of merchandise to a customer could not scale without machine-aided predictions and recommendations at the level of the individual customer. But the process also requires a human in the middle (between the machine prediction and the customer) to provide the personal support and customer relationship to make this subscription model work.

Hybrid Augmentation

Of course, not everything is black and white—shades of gray are often the norm. Therefore, it is not surprising that in many situations, an organization will want to use a combination of weak and strong augmentation to support the same set of processes. This hybrid approach is required when implemented business models change. It is possible to automate simple manual tasks in the context of an overall redesign. To understand how these different approaches to intelligent augmentation work, we will delve deeper into what is needed to transform businesses. Let's consider these approaches as ways to best leverage human and machine capabilities together within a business process for achieving the best results.

Summary

Applying augmented intelligence to a business process is a path to process improvement. The type of improvement depends on the approach taken:

- **Weak Augmentation:** In this approach, several steps or tasks of an existing business process are automated without changing the workflow of the process itself. This technique is well suited to repetitive transactional processes, such as invoice handling. These processes typically feature routine but labor-intensive tasks such as filling out a set of forms and documents. Robotic process automation can be applied selectively to several tasks, reducing the cost and improving accuracy for the end-to-end process. Measuring the costs to run the process before the automation is implemented sets a baseline against which the post-implementation process costs can be compared.

- **Strong Augmentation:** In this approach, the task flow in the process is redesigned so that the work is done in a new way via machine–human collaboration. This technique is well suited to processes that involve judgment, such as deciding on what to offer an individual customer using knowledge of their preferences. Machine-generated predictions and recommendations enable this process to scale with humans applying judgment to review and adjust the recommendation. This approach can yield higher revenues. Setting up a benchmark for before-and-after comparisons is important.

- **Business Model Change:** This hybrid approach goes beyond process improvement but seeks to change the fundamental business model of the organization through the application of augmented intelligence. The goal is to deliver goods or services in a new way, which becomes the firm's competitive advantage.

These scenarios for augmented intelligence are not mutually exclusive. An organization can take advantage of weak augmentation, which substitutes machines for human labor for simpler, routine tasks. The result can drive down costs. With strong augmentation, tasks involving judgment can be improved via machine-generated predictions. The resulting recommendations can be reviewed by human agents, with the goal of driving top-line increases to revenues. as needed. Finally, the biggest potential is for an organization to revise their core business models, finding new ways to deliver goods and services via human–machine collaboration, which provides a competitive advantage in the marketplace. The most advanced organizations utilize all three of these augmented intelligence strategies.

Chapter 6

Risks in Augmented Intelligence

Introduction

The commercialization of machine learning (ML) models and artificial intelligence (AI) is bringing about a dramatic transformation in the way businesses view the value of their data. Although there is no doubt that there is incredible potential, this era represents a challenging transition time for businesses and technology leaders. Amid all the potential benefits of AI and ML, there are serious risks that often are ignored. Organizations must be able to deal with an abundance of both business and technical risks. Some risks are obvious, such as the ethical risks of collecting personal data when individuals have not given their permission. However, business leaders need to understand the vast array of risks and issues they need to prepare for before they can leverage the power of AI and ML.

In this chapter, we discuss risks that businesses need to consider when applying machine learning to business tasks that have the potential to augment how work gets accomplished in everyday business life. We are separating risks from the ethical issues of gathering data. The issue of ethics and governance will be discussed in Chapter 7. In Chapter 7, we discuss the potential for litigation stemming from ethical failures that impact customers' lives and finances.

Providing Context and Understanding

Before we get into the details of the risks a business needs to be prepared to address, let's take a step back and understand what is actually happening inside the machine learning components as they apply to business tasks. Let's assume that a business plans to replace straightforward repetitive process tasks with machine learning models. Although there are wild promises that machines will be smart enough to replace everything a human does, it is not quite that simple—even when the tasks seem relatively routine. For example, the machine learning model would have to learn the purpose and context is for every task being automated. What is the goal of executing a process? What happens if an action related to one task is done incorrectly because of a problem with the data that has been ingested? What if the data is old and hasn't been updated? What if two different processes are using different data sources and different conflicting rules? Unlike a human team member, an ML component cannot alert other team members about the job it performs, or work around activities if something seems wrong.

Furthermore, we can ask: Do the results of the process really serve the business objectives of the organization? Remember that ML algorithms and models are code created by developers. Successful models require enough knowledge and nuance from the team of experts to ensure that the results are correct and useful for the business task. If the developer does not understand the business and the processes behind the way the business should operate, the models are likely to fail to achieve their goals and add a significant level of risk to the organization.

Once a machine learning component is available to perform a business task without a team member, the way the business process is executed will have to change. At a fundamental level, there are simply different expectations for how automation handles a problem compared to how a person will approach the same task. In the traditional business, staff members have a set process for conducting business and rarely alter their routine unless forced to by changing business conditions. Needless to say, people are creatures of habit. In contrast, a machine learning model is not bound by "the way things have always been done." One of the powerful characteristics of a machine learning model is that it is capable of creating an innovative approach to achieving a business objective. The objective of the model requires that business processes must evolve so that they are more efficient, more adaptable, and more innovative. But there is a danger in simply trusting a machine to understand the constraints required for a responsible business. So, the question remains, how do you innovate and transform without putting the business at risk?

Building an innovative model is not automatic. The data scientist must work side by side with subject matter experts to understand the purpose of the business process and how it can be changed and adapted in a consistent and predictable manner. If the team builds a model in isolation, it is possible to create unanticipated consequences that risk real harm to the business. For example, consider a business process that requires the business to guarantee that if a product is not in stock, the company will offer the customer a third-party alternative if they agree. What if the ML model that predicts product availability fails to include the permission agreement? In this case, a tried-and-true business process has violated the trust between vendor and customer. Failure to support this adaptation and provide it with sufficient resources assures that the augmentation of the team will fail or perform poorly.

The Human Factor

It is tempting to assume that once a business builds a machine learning component, the staff's job is done. The process may have been directly automated or even dramatically changed. However, this simplistic view does not consider some key considerations. First, let's assume that the process has been completely redesigned so that there is no historical data available for testing. This new process has to be integrated with the rest of the overall business process that operates a key part of how business is conducted. The machine only executes the model based on the data being ingested. The model often must be viewed as part of a larger unit of work that defines a combination of new innovations and basic best practices for an industry. Although digital disruption is a rallying cry for businesses that need to change to compete, there are certain business principles of how commerce is conducted that will never change. For example, the customer must be provided with the right level of information to ensure the accountability of the vendor. The product and service must be delivered at the right time and the right price. Accounts payable (AP) processes have to work as required by the company's business practices.

The basic truth is that the human team still understands the context of the organization's overall business process. It is critical that team members be able to quickly manage important changes to business processes as the market changes. It may not be obvious how the ML component will impact a business process. All team members, not just the data scientist and subject experts, need to know how the ML model is intended to work and where it fits into the overall process. Then they can assess if the model is contributing to the business process changes and whether the changes are having the intended goals. If the model is not contributing well, then the team will need to step, document the failures, and make changes in the model. Therefore, the model has to be designed to anticipate errors and the fact that customers do not always act rationally.

Understanding the Risks of a ML Model

How do you know how well a machine learning model is performing? Is it the responsibility of senior managers? Does the data scientist have the ability to understand what is happening within that model? In reality, many risks can impact the validity and consequences of deploying a model. What if the data scientist has selected an algorithm that is not appropriate for the task at hand? What if the algorithm is not given enough data? There may be a situation when the wrong features (measurable property) are selected. Selecting a wrong feature can mean that the wrong characteristic is being measured and, therefore, will not be helpful to the business. The risk of wrong feature selection can be significant because management will pay attention to the wrong processes and issues. Even if the features are correct, the model's performance may be hindered by the new data being ingested into the model. When data is not correct, the business process simply will fail to deliver the required business results.

A new ML component is a bit like a new employee who seems to have all the right credentials for the job but is unable to fulfill the needs of the business. The employee might have potential but may not understand the business well enough to make the right decisions. Likewise, as the business adopts new business processes based on changed machine learning models, there is a risk that the model will not perform as intended and cause problems. An even more dangerous risk is that the process in which the model does its work will be compromised. Therefore, both the data scientists and the business team members have to understand the components of the model well enough to be able to assess the performance of the model with the ingested data and how it is impacting the overall business processes in which it operates. The team must regularly check that the model is doing what it is expected to do and have a means of performing digital audits, that is, simply said, running tests to ensure that the model is working well.

The Importance of Digital Auditing

One technique that has emerged to help is to have experts conduct digital auditing to assess how well an algorithmic model is working. That assessment is called algorithmic accountability. Algorithmic accountability is not just good "business hygiene." It is essential for knowing that models coming from machine learning algorithms work properly, and for conforming with new federal laws being developed by the US Congress to address machine learning and its role in business.

Although outside consulting firms are now offering special services for digital auditing, this process can be managed in house if senior management engages a business to undertake this process. Digital auditing involves assessment of what goals the algorithm has been asked to address, what decisions it is making, and what data has been used to create the model decisions. The whole process of developing the algorithmic model, including the training and testing of the model, must be scrutinized to assure that the model has not introduced bias in its decision making.

Algorithm accountability will be even more useful if the tests that make up a digital audit use both past as well as new business data (even if the team has to "make up" the data because there is none at hand). Because the needs of customers evolve over time, those changes will be reflected in the data the business inputs to the model. If new data is markedly different from the original data used to build the model, then the algorithm could make different decisions given the new data. Assessing the model's performance on old and new data will give some indication of the overall behavior of the model.

Furthermore, some knowledge of the differences in the use of new data will allow the team to continually assess whether the model is changing or instead failing, as more and more new data come online. The value of new data is its use in seeing new trends before human teams become aware of them. However, if there is not enough new data to retrain the model, the old model will hold sway and make fewer good predictions. If there is enough new data and the new results are dramatically different, the model might seem unreliable to the team. It is imperative to keep the team informed about how well an algorithm is performing in order to mitigate risks in using machine learning–based models.

Other factors can be critical in digital auditing. Not only can a machine learning algorithm be faulty, but efforts to correct predictions can be suppressed. For example, a model's predictions might be ignored if it surfaces problems in product safety that the team does not want to acknowledge. Correct predictions could also be manipulated to add results that favor a direction desired by some part of the management team. Although overall digital auditing goes beyond the concerns of AI augmentation, its practice will be valuable to many businesses in mitigating the risks in machine learning models.

The Risks in Capturing More Data

Many companies are beginning to use powerful machine learning techniques as a way to transform their business processes. Leveraging data in order to drive business decisions through artificial intelligence and machine learning models can be surprisingly powerful. However, teams may rush to begin using machine learning models without understanding the full impact on the business. One of the biggest issues that organizations face is that they simply do not have enough data to ensure the accuracy of results from the use of machine learning algorithms. Gathering an ample amount of data often requires procuring information from partners or other third-party data sources. Sharing this data can result in exposing private customer data. The typical process of anonymizing data is intended to sanitize private information. Anonymizing is done either through encryption or by removing personally identifiable information from data. Masking company data for others to use is challenging and risky. First, the business has to be very careful that critical private or mission critical data isn't accidently disclosed. Although experienced security experts are often able to protect data, there are no guarantees that mistakes will not occur. Avoiding risks of data security breaches requires a team effort to ensure that everyone understands the rules: what data must be kept private and what data can be freely shared. It is not surprising that a number of businesses simply refuse to share data that they consider too private and confidential to expose the information outside their data center. The risks may not even with obvious. For example, there have been situations in which business leaders did not even realize that data rules have been violated. For example, there was a situation at a state governmental agency where data scientists were analyzing citizen data. All social security numbers and names were blacked out. However, there was enough other identifiable information that it was easy to determine the identities of individuals.

Why It Is Hard to Manage Risk

Although it is impossible to anticipate all the risks that can result from the way data is used within machine learning models, there are some fundamental risks that are a good starting point. In this next section we will detail seven important risks that should help you get started. Keep in mind that as you work with your models in context with business change, new risks may emerge.

Seven Key Risks

If you are not prepared to deal with risks, you will be putting your business in danger. One of the ironic factors leading to these risks is that you are innovating by beginning to break down silos between your sources of data.

1. The Risk of Overfitting or Underfitting

We have talked a lot in this book about the problem presented by either overfitting or underfitting data when used with machine learning algorithms. This problem occurs when the data is not good enough to be able to successfully predict outcomes from business processes. The risk is simply that the ML component will predict outcomes poorly and thereby negatively affect the business process it is meant to enhance. The work of the business managers taking on the use of ML components in their business is to understand enough about the data science teams' efforts or to seek outside consultant advice to be reasonably convinced that efforts in collecting and using data are sound. Everyone knows there are no guarantees for anything in the world, but business managers must use every knowledge resource at their disposal to mitigate the risks associated with data and its use in ML algorithms.

To mitigate this risk, a strong team of ML data scientists working in collaboration with team members who have a deep understanding of business processes should be able to avoid using inappropriate data sets. Collaboration is key in this effort because each team member must understand the roles of the other members. Furthermore, they must combine their individual experiences to assess the data sets and problems being addressed. Although there are no guarantees of success, the team that works together and understands the value of all its members stands the best chance of succeeding.

2. Changing Business Processes Increases Risk

As you change business processes and begin to leverage machine learning to study the discontinuities in your business operations, you will introduce new risks. Typically, employees follow well-understood processes, even if they are inefficient or even harmful to the business. It is hard to change habits that have often been in place for many years. If the staff is unwilling to adapt to new processes or they don't understand what they are being asked to do, you may be setting the organization up for failure. As a consequence, staff members who are adopting new processes may avoid following new procedures or make decisions that are contrary to what the data indicates.

Mitigating the risk of employees derailing changes to the process requires the skills of experienced managers to motivate employees to adapt and spearhead changes in business processes. In addition, successful managers will motivate teams to learn how ML models can be used effectively.

3. The Risk of Bias

In previous chapters, we have discussed the fact that bias can exist in the data used in building a model. Bias is a significant business risk because it leads to incorrect model predictions about customer needs, about the nature of one's customers, or about the products a business is developing. Bias is potentially debilitating to a business in two major ways.

- *Failure to Understand the Ethical Implications:* Bias can lead to ethical and legal challenges discussed further in Chapter 7. The promise of the machine learning model is being able to conduct advanced analysis that can provide you with important insights that were not possible by reviewing the data manually. However, if the data used causes the model to produce results that harm a protected group (e.g., the aged, the disabled, or ethnic groups), by charging them more for services, excluding them from services or products, or limiting their participation in the business, your business itself incurs a large risk: The business itself is seen both ethically and legally as biased against that special group and can face all the legal challenges that come with such a view.
- *The Risk of Poor Business Decisions:* In an era of excitement around artificial intelligence, it is not surprising that data scientists and business leaders would fall in love with algorithms as a way to analyze data that helps make critical business decisions. The key risks that arise from the use of machine learning–based models include biases that might be unintentional and harmful to the business as a business.

Algorithms are vulnerable to risks, such as accidental or intentional biases, errors, and frauds. Catching biases is essential because biased decisions can lead to poor business decisions that will hurt future growth. What is the impact of bias? Here are some examples that could impact your organization:

- Leaving out a critical population of customers.
- Producing product offerings that ignore a group of important customers.
- Discounting the knowledge of a business team that has operated successfully in the past.
- Encouraging business decisions that favor an old process because new approaches are not reflected in the existing data used to create the model. Even the decision about employees can be compromised. Companies that use ML models to decide who to interview for employment risk bias in choosing employees similar to the ones they have. They will miss out on employees with new ideas and new energy!

Biases that harm businesses are different from the ones that leave out protected populations and lead to ethical and legal challenges. However, these biases harm the business by causing decisions that neglect new customer groups, discount successful internal teams, or ignore potential new products and exclude new processes that could further enhance a company's goals. If your data models are biased, you put your business at risk.

How Can the Risk of Bias Be Mitigated?

There are no tried-and-true methods for eliminating bias in the data used to create ML-based models. This challenge of biases in data is currently the source of a significant amount of research in the field of data science. In the meantime, a machine learning–based model for a part of your business cannot and should not replace brainstorming and smart thinking on the part of your business teams. To aid in these efforts, a business team should ask itself several questions: Do the predictions of the model seem fair to all the customer segments on which it operates? Are there new products and services we think might become a trend that are not predicted by this model? Are there new company goals that this model is not addressing? Smart thinking and creative answers by the human team mean that machine learning models can augment the business as well as illustrate why the human team is still so critical to business.

4. The Risk of Over Relying on the Algorithm

Creating machine learning models can lead a business team to rely on the algorithm without hesitation. Because it is hard work to create a model, and once it looks like the model works well, it's tempting to allow the model to work without human intervention. However, this tactic risks a model that will not behave as expected and will make poor decisions.

How can this risk be mitigated? As we have pointed out previously, a model must be carefully vetted before it is put into practice, and must be reviewed periodically. Initial vetting requires training the model on part of the available data and then testing it on a different part of the data. When doing initial tests, the results, usually given as percentages of correct choices, must be high enough that the team feels confident in dealing with whatever percentage of mistakes the model makes. Periodic reviews of a working model prevent the model from making choices because it has become out of date due to new data that has not been incorporated in the model. The business team must make periodic reviews because otherwise the team will not have a way of noticing if the model is beginning to fail.

5. The Risk of Lack of Explainability

With the exception of models that are the product of decision trees (which are not widely used by data scientists, as discussed in Chapter 4), the models created by machine learning algorithms come without any explanation of how they made their decisions—that is, machine learning algorithms are a black box that no one can look inside of. If you can't look inside the box, how can you know why the model makes the decisions it does? The answer is simply that there is no direct way to know.

The Model Lacks Explainability

This lack of explanation is a major drawback to using ML-based models. There are two key risks involved in the lack of explainability. First, business teams won't use the models because they do not know how they made their decisions and cannot be sure they work as advertised. Second, no one can explain to customers, lawyers, or auditors why the model made the decision it did, except to say that the decision results from patterns in the data that the ML algorithm found and fixed into the model. Put in this light, it sounds very risky to rely on models that cannot be explained.

How can a business team mitigate this risk? Principally, the team needs to be able to carefully test the model to begin with so that it behaves as expected. At this point, the model needs to be periodically reviewed so that algorithms can be updated as needed. Once an algorithmic model is up and running, the team must test the model carefully to see that it is operating in a reasonable way. This requires a different level of testing than was conducted before the model was put into production. This new level of testing is based on the experience of team members to assess just what the model is doing and to determine if the outcomes make sense. The challenge in this risk mitigation is to determine the line between reasonable predictions that may point in new directions and unreasonable predictions that are a result of faulty data. The team is responsible for capturing subtleties, nuances, and context in order to mitigate risk.

6. The Risk of Revealing Confidential Information

Often, machine learning systems ingest personal data that must be kept confidential. While masking can be used as a technique to keep information such as social security numbers private, there are risks. For example, it is possible to take all of the data that has not been masked and determine the identity of an individual. In reality, anonymizing data is complex. For example, let's say an organization is analyzing voting records. Information about the name of the person is masked. However, analyzing all of the other fields makes it relatively easy to figure out identities. However, removing additional data to try to reduce risk will result in a data set that is useless because it is devoid of meaningful information. There are situations in which a data scientist grabs a lot of data to test and train a model not realizing that the selected data has sensitive information that should not be revealed.

How can the risk of revealing confidential information be mitigated? In the data-gathering process, the business team building the ML models must review the data being offered for the ML algorithm and eliminate any data the team feels might be problematic. When a team is aggregating several fields of data, it is their responsibility to determine if portions of the data reveal confidential data. These reviews are not easy to undertake and provide no guarantees, but they are essential to the risk management process.

7. The Risk of a Poorly Constructed Team

An organization can hire the most talented data scientists but end up with a failed effort. The data scientists can build a model that really does not help to solve a business process problem. How can you recreate business processes with machine learning models that take into account the subtle nuances of business operations? Is there adequate knowledge of current and changing business models? These are difficult questions, and failing to answer them well can result in risks to the effort to use machine learning models.

To mitigate this risk, it is necessary to create a team consisting of (1) business experts who have experience in the business processes that might be changed with machine learning and who understand the value and role of machine learning models, and (2) data scientists who can build machine learning models and who are willing to learn about the business from their business counterparts. In a perfect world, it would be possible to find team members who have both in-depth business expertise and data science knowledge. Central to this risk mitigation, business leaders and data scientists have to be willing to collaborate. The team must undertake the collaborations with openness to new perspectives outside of their comfort zones.

Summary

Machine learning models for business decision making are incredibly powerful in helping subject matter experts gain better insights into the steps needed to execute decisions. Being able to harness all of the data collected over years to find patterns and anomalies is powerful but not without risk. If an organization approaches machine learning with a focus on avoiding pitfalls, the models can be a game changer.

This chapter has presented seven key risks for businesses using machine learning models to enhance business decision making: overfitting or underfitting the data used in the model, changing business processes, failure to understand the ethical implications in biases in data and models, poor business decisions based on bias, overreliance on the machine learning model, lack of explainability of the model, revealing confidential information in sharing data for models, and constructing a team with little regard for their skill and knowledge in using the model. Each of these risks can be significantly mitigated by awareness of these risks by a team of business and machine learning experts chosen to work on business processes, including the machine learning models, along with regular review of the data used in the model as well as the model's performance. In addition, the business team should take the time to brainstorm new ways to deal with changes in the model as the business strategy transitions.

Chapter 7

The Criticality of Governance and Ethics in Augmented Intelligence

Introduction

When organizations begin to leverage their critical data, there is often a rush to quickly gain insights. Therefore, it is not surprising that data scientists and knowledge experts will focus on gathering and cleansing data and building models. Issues such as governance and ethics often take a back seat. The issues of governance and ethics only take center stage when there are incidents that land on the front page of the business press. Governance cannot be an afterthought when moving to augmented intelligence, since it must combine corporate and government-mandated processes and data tied to organizational requirements. Governance must also focus on the ethics of how a company behaves in terms of protecting its customers. It is the responsibility of both corporate and IT management to monitor activities to ensure that rules are followed. If governance and ethics are ignored, a company's reputation will be badly tarnished and financial consequences can be significant. In this chapter, we discuss the need to apply governance rules and ethical business practices to support your data.

Defining a Control Framework

To establish a consistent and predictable way to govern your data and your models, it is imperative to put a governance control framework in place. Simply put, you must focus on the controls you need to put in place to protect your business and your customers. A control framework creates the basis for formulating policies and procedures for working with data, machine learning (ML) and augmented intelligence. Your augmented intelligence control framework should be enforced throughout the business. Adherence to this control framework has to be designed in at every stage of implementation—from the pilot to full-blown implementation.

When you begin to think about controls over your data, you need to consider a number of different controls that apply to your entire data cycle. Managing the data cycle requires that controls apply across the entire data cycle:

- Controls should govern the way data is acquired, protecting data privacy by ensuring consumer opt in—both for the data items collected and any derived data.
- Controls should govern the breadth of the data collected, to limit the risk of training a machine to perpetuate the bias built into the record of current practice.
- Controls should ensure transparency in the model, sufficient to yield an explanation of the factors that drive the model's recommendation.

For purchased algorithms, a business cannot ensure that any of these principles were followed when the model was developed. In such a case, controls need to be applied before a model's recommendation is put into action. Likewise, when you purchase third-party data, you must ensure that proper controls were in place during the collection of that data.

To create your framework, you need to bring together teams from across your business. It is important to include both legal and compliance teams, but you should also include business executives. There are data governance and control rules that you are legally obligated to follow. For example, if you are a credit card company, you cannot include certain types of data in your creditworthiness algorithm. Certain data features about an individual, such as ethnicity, cannot be used. Your compliance and legal teams will outline data features that are barred from use. There are other data features that require your business to decide how they should be factored into an algorithm. Let's look at the issue of gender. Depending on your business, it may be prudent to factor gender into an algorithm. For example, it's well known that auto insurance rates are higher for young men than young women because young men have higher claims rates.

Likewise, nobody is going to argue that a health and beauty company should market products differently to different genders: Men and women obviously use very different grooming products.

But things are not as simple as they may seem at first glance. There are a number of nuances that organizations must consider in order to both market correctly and not run into compliance and ethical issues. For example, the biological differences between males and females would factor into the health and beauty market and necessitate not just different marketing campaigns but different products. However, a marketing plan designed to offer women toothpaste that is packaged in a pink box will likely be ineffective and deliver no real value. Although an insurance company may use statistical data to price insurance based on the fact that men may have more accidents than women, there are men with certain characteristics who actually have fewer accidents than women. If a man who has no accidents is charged more than women who have been involved in a number of accidents, this pricing scheme may be viewed as biased.

Let's revisit the original example of the credit card issuer. We can all agree that race should not be a factor when deciding an individual's creditworthiness. In fact, the Federal Trade Commission (FTC) enforces the United State's Equal Credit Opportunity Act (ECOA). The ECOA prohibits credit discrimination on the basis of race, color, religion, national origin, sex, marital status, age, or because you get public assistance. However, these factors might slip into an ML creditworthiness application through a back door. Let's look at age. If a prospective customer's high school or college graduation date is used as part of a company's creditworthiness algorithm, the system may begin to disfavor new graduates who also tend to be younger applicants. Similarly, if you begin to drill down into the credit applicants' four-digit zip code and include demographic data about that specific area, issues like race and national origin may creep into your determination on creditworthiness. These types of problems are why it is so important to have a cross-functional team create an AI control framework.

Technologists must be part of the team in order to fully explain the types of data that is being analyzed and why it is being included in the model. In many cases, machine learning algorithms are black boxes, and it is nearly impossible to understand exactly how a feature pertaining to a protected class is being factored into the model. One step that companies are implementing is to incorporate a testing procedure in which you check the output of the model to determine if the results favor a particular race, gender, or other category of people. This sort of testing is one of the steps that can be built into your governance framework before any model is put into production. Business and compliance teams can then question the need to include certain data factors and the possible pitfalls and concerns of including that information. Furthermore, the business teams and business executives will need to determine if they are comfortable using certain data features in an algorithm. The business team needs to decide if including certain data features in its calculations goes against the corporate ethos, or corporate ethics. Even if a company puts profits above any sort of ethics, the business team must still consider the possible risks of including certain features in a model. For example, a restaurant loyalty program is not legally barred from including factors such as race, marital status, and gender into their rewards program. An analytics team might determine that a model can be made slightly more accurate by including such features about customers. However, if the public finds out that those factors are impacting their rewards points, there could be outrage. It is easy to imagine the headlines, protests, and boycotts that would surely follow the discovery.

YouTube's Engagement Model Can Spawn Ethical and Governance Problems

Like any ad-supported Internet platform, Google's YouTube has a goal of keeping users engaged and on its page for as long as possible. The longer a user is on YouTube, the more ads they can be shown. To further this goal, as somebody watches a video, YouTube suggests additional videos that the customer is likely to click on. As it turns out, YouTube viewers have a very high propensity to click on conspiracy-theory videos. For example, if someone is researching the moon landing, the YouTube algorithm would determine that the individual is likely to click on a video claiming that the moon landing was faked. This can lead to a spiral of being served more and more content claiming that the US government or other agencies faked all of the Apollo missions. Although the user may have originally just wanted to spend 10 minutes seeing footage from the moon, they may have spent two hours "learning" about how the moon landing was faked.

Of course, for YouTube's business, this is a great win: They were able to keep the user engaged on their platform for a prolonged amount of time (user engagement is one of the key factors that investors like to evaluate). On the other hand, YouTube has begun to recognize the problem of spreading disinformation. The company is changing its algorithms to help stop the spread of non–fact-based conspiracies.[1] In addition to altering its algorithms, YouTube is also using human reviewers to help better train the models that suggest videos and censor content. Although this decision might hurt the company's time of engagement, the decision was made at high levels because executives determined that the pushing of conspiracies conflicts with the company's ethics, or that the negative headlines were bad for business.

Creating Your Augmented Intelligence Control Framework

A good way to start off your framework is to think about the types of data you will include in your models and the possible use cases. This first step begins to create your *control environment*. The control environment provides the foundational internal rules and guidelines on how different types of data can be used. There is almost a limitless number of use cases and types of data, but why don't we look at how this assessment might look for a travel company. Figure 7-1 depicts a chart in which types of data are on the vertical axis and use cases are on the horizontal axis. Guidelines on how data should be used in an AI project are in the corresponding boxes. Of course, this is just a simple example, and

	Initial Marketing	Pricing	Upselling
Customer gender	Create campaigns targeting different activities.	Do not factor.	Promote different excursions or activities.
Does the customer have children?	Campaigns focused on family-friendly activities.	Perhaps you want to create options for less expensive travel for children.	Promote different excursions or activities.
Customer income	Campaigns based on the type of travel that the customer would likely book (i.e., budget vs. luxury travel).	Do not factor.	Offer unique, custom options for high-net customers, whereas more budget-focused travelers can be offered smaller upgrades for a low cost.
Weather where customer is located	Create a custom campaign when certain weather events occur.	Sales based on current weather where customers are located.	Opportunities to reach out to customers who have already booked but might be impacted by current weather. Example: Customer is experiencing a blizzard but has an upcoming trip to the Caribbean—offer them a half-day boat excursion to a deserted beach.
Customer loyalty to your brand	Treat your loyal customers wonderfully, and promote the perks of being loyal.	Loyal customers may receive discounts.	Maybe your most loyal customers get certain perks and discounts on special opportunities.

Figure 7-1 Factors to Consider in Governing Different Types of Data

your guidelines will be more complex as you bring together the opinions of data scientists and business leadership, along with the legal and compliance teams.

You can quickly see how this type of chart would be very different for a company that must comply with the Equal Credit Opportunity Act or other similar regulations. In addition, there are other factors that you might want to bar teams from ever considering (i.e., race, sexual orientation, political affiliation, etc.).

Steps in Your AI Control Framework

There are a number of steps required to control your data so that it meets both your governance and ethical requirements. These steps include conducting a risk assessment, creating control activities, and creating a monitoring system.

Conducting a Risk Assessment

The first step to create your control framework is to perform a *risk assessment*. You must determine the potential risks your organization faces as you continue down your AI journey. Even if you are following regulatory and compliance requirements, what are the social implications that you need to consider? Later in this chapter we talk about several use cases in which companies do not breach legal requirements, but their algorithms go beyond the comfort level of most people. You must also think about the level of notice customers and prospects receive regarding how their data will be used. Is the disclosure on how data will be used on page 4 of a terms and conditions agreement that nobody reads? If you sell customer or prospect data, do you have any controls over how that data is used in the future? If you do have policies regarding how customer data can be used by third parties, how do you ensure that those policies are being enforced? If you buy third-party data from other sources, are you sure that the data meets your own internal controls? Was that data lawfully collected? All of these risks must be considered by your cross-functional team.

Creating Control Activities

The next step in the creation of your augmented intelligence control framework is to create *control activities*. These are specific rules, policies, and procedures that are established to make sure that business units are following your agreed-upon data rules. For example, you may want to institute special rules when a group wants to use gender in a machine learning algorithm. The rule might say that if gender is to be used when creating a model, the data team must get approval from a senior manager in the corresponding business unit. It is then up to that manager to approve, disapprove, or loop in compliance teams. This rule can be codified into the model-building process to create guardrails so that teams stay safe from violating established controls. If a manager receives a request to use gender in a marketing campaign, they will likely quickly approve of the use. On the other hand, if it is a human resources (HR) use case, the manager may need to disapprove of it or bring in legal and compliance colleagues to help determine the appropriateness of using gender.

Creating a Monitoring System

The final step in creating your control framework is to create a *monitoring system*. Many businesses that are experiencing successful implementations of AI have internal monitoring systems to make sure that internal controls are being followed. Monitoring should be overseen by executives who have two important mandates—(1) financial success; and (2) preventing avoidable risks, embarrassment, and legal problems. These executives should be well versed in the company's risk tolerance and the values that the company believes in: A family-friendly brand is going to have a very different risk tolerance than a company solely focused on males in the 18- to 40-year-old demographic. The executives that are overseeing the monitoring process do not need to understand the bits and bytes of your company's AI algorithms and models. Instead, they need to work with data teams who can explain the types of data that are going into a model, how data is being collected, and the impact of including different types of data in a model. If using age in a model only gives a very slight lift to a model's accuracy, the executive might determine that it doesn't make sense, from a risk perspective, to include age in the model.

Data Privacy Controls

If the business needs to acquire additional customer data, it can reach out to customers and obtain their permission to gather additional data about them. The company can also acquire additional attributes (i.e., features) about its customers. Having additional attributes available for model building can enhance the model's predictive power. It is increasingly easy for businesses to enrich their customer and prospect data with various third-party data sources. For example, they can match a customer's information with that customer's social media data.

The business can also shop for data from specialized data brokers who possess data on individuals who are not customers. It has been a common practice

The Ethics of Using Data to Modulate Pricing

Similar to any mobile application, users of Uber grant the company permission to access a lot of data. Buried in the terms and conditions of Uber's app is a condition that gives the company the right to see your phone's battery percentage. In a May 17, 2016, interview on NPR's podcast Hidden Brain, Keith Chen, former head of economic research at Uber and current Associate Professor of Economics at UCLA Anderson was interviewed.[2] During the interview, Chen revealed that Uber users are more likely to pay for surge pricing if the battery on their phone is low. Rather than waiting for surge pricing to go down, or trying to quit the app and restart it to see if the pricing has changed, the user has a high propensity to just accept the high pricing. Clearly, Uber could use this type of data to maximize its revenue and run tests to see how much they can charge before a large amount of low battery customers seek out alternative systems. When asked whether the company takes advantage of this data, Chen made it clear that Uber does not, stating that "We absolutely don't use that to kind of like push you a higher surge price, but it's an interesting kind of psychological fact of human behavior."

This is an example of corporate ethics and risks. Although it would look terrible if there was a news story about Uber gouging users whose batteries were low, few people would argue with a hotel incorporating status at other chains into their pricing model. If a traveler is a platinum member at a certain hotel brand, it makes sense for a competing brand to offer aggressive discounting, upgrades, or automatic platinum-status matching.

in marketing to acquire email lists or to access consumer data on social media sites such as Google, Facebook, or LinkedIn. Businesses now must be aware of enhanced regulatory controls on data privacy when reaching out to consumers via acquired data. Permission must be granted from the consumer to use the data via an opt-in process. But gaining such permission is difficult if there is no preexisting relationship between a business and the consumer.

There are now further challenges with the opt-in process that are becoming apparent. The very definition of "opt in" must be considered as well. Many individuals do not fully appreciate the implications of opting in. Additionally, if you want to use a service, or enter a store's premises, you may have no option but to opt in. There are several well-publicized cases that have raised questions on the adequacy of opt-in mechanisms to provide transparency to consumers on how a business is using their personal data. Here are two examples.

In one case, a predictive model was built for the retailer Target to determine whether a customer was likely to be pregnant. The model based its predictions on an analysis of retail transactions captured in point-of-sale data. Women who became pregnant tended to significantly change their purchase patterns. Armed with this knowledge, the retailer sent coupons for baby and maternity products to each consumer flagged by the model. The marketing campaign caused a furor when it was reported that a father first learned that his teenage daughter was pregnant after Target's mail offers to his daughter raised his suspicions.[3] This chain of events was not envisioned by the consumer when she gave permission for the retailer to access her point-of-sale data.

A second case involved the collection of data on Facebook users (and their friends) via an app built on the Facebook platform for Cambridge Analytica and then downloaded by Facebook users. The personal and social data collected was used to target voters on behalf of the Trump campaign in the 2016 US presidential election.[4]

In both the Target and the Cambridge Analytica cases, customer opt in did not provide sufficient transparency to the consumers about how their personal data would be used by developers and advertisers:

- Consumers were not informed that additional personal data would be derived via algorithms from the data for which they had provided opt-in approval. In the Target example, this practice was especially problematic, since the derived data was protected health data.
- Consumers were not informed about which types of actions would be taken based on the derived personal data. And they were not informed about who would be acting on the data, whether it was a retailer or a political campaign.

Additionally, consumers were not informed that access to their personal data could be granted because a friend had granted access to his/her personal network. In the Facebook situation, access to a user's data brought access to data on the user's network of friends. This shift from personal data to social data raises additional privacy questions, which are being studied by government officials in Europe and the United States. New government regulations are establishing new standards on data privacy. The European Union (EU) leads this effort. General Data Protection Regulation (GDPR) was passed in 2016, and its enforcement phase began in May 2018. Likewise, in June 2018, the California Consumer Privacy Act, influenced by GDPR, was passed. This state regulation institutes the strongest privacy laws in the United States.

These new data privacy regulations are adding friction to the process of acquiring personal and social data and then acting on this customer data. The new regulations will require businesses to take several new areas into account:

- **Right to consent:** The opt-in process needs to be made more transparent and more specific to consumers. This calls into question today's practice of requesting a general opt in by a consumer for any and all uses of his or her personal data collected by a business. More granular permission will be required in the future, getting an opt in for specific data and for specific actions that could be taken by the business. The consent request should be clear, and the consumer should have ready access to view all consent requests that have been granted. A growing number of consumers are demanding that businesses and websites show them all the personal data that has been collected.

- **Right to be forgotten and the right to erasure:** The right to be forgotten has a long history in the legal system as protection for people seeking to expunge their past records from public view. With today's widespread use of search engines, this has come to include the deletion of URLs from search results. But GDPR goes further to specifically demand a right to erasure. As a practical matter, businesses as well as Internet social media or search companies will need to respond to a consumer request to delete all personal data.

- **Right to an explanation:** When algorithms are used for making decisions about consumers, a consumer can demand to know the reasons for the decision. They can request to know which factors were considered by the algorithm when the decision was made. This principle is well established in the field of credit scoring, where there are long-standing regulations that require the credit-scoring company to list the key factors that impacted the score. More recently, GDPR speaks of a broader "right to an explanation" for a decision, though its scope and specific application is not yet settled. This right seeks to address issues of alleged algorithmic bias, sometimes referred to as "algorithmic redlining." This right extends to areas such as hiring, the granting of mortgage loans, and the sentencing of defendants. The implication for an organization is that it must be able to provide a level of transparency as to which factors drove the algorithmic recommendation or decision.

On an Organizational Approach to Controls

A variety of new governance and ethical requirements are shining a light on the role of data in today's organization. It's imperative for organizations to develop well-thought-out policies on how data is collected, managed, and used. At the same time, it's imperative for individuals to monitor what permissions they have granted for the use of their personal data and to demand greater transparency on future use. This awareness demands a response from organizations to develop policies that govern data use so that they can maintain the trust of their customers, as well as staying ahead of emerging legal standards.

GDPR Requires You to Rethink Your Control Framework

Large enterprises and multinational businesses have had to think about how GDPR will impact their business. Businesses have always had to walk a fine line between gathering and analyzing massive amounts of customer and prospect data and keeping private data and secure from both regulatory and reputational standpoints. What's different about GDPR is that it will impose substantial financial penalties if a company fails to comply with the regulation: Companies risk fines of up to four percent of their annual global revenue.

GDPR specifies eight rights that apply to citizens regarding the use of their data by external organizations:

1. Right to be informed[5, 6]
2. The right of access[7]
3. The right to rectification[8]
4. The right to erasure[9]
5. The right to restrict processing[10]
6. The right to data portability[11]
7. The right to object[12]
8. Rights in relation to automated decision making and profiling[13]

It is important to keep in mind that GDPR is not the only data protection regulation. The California Consumer Privacy Act that goes into effect January 1, 2020, will put greater restrictions around how companies can collect and use data. Regulations are constantly evolving. As compliance, legal, technical, and security teams work to ready their organizations for these rules, they must keep an eye on the future, anticipating new requirements that may impact the business.

Best Practices for Ensuring Data Privacy and Security

How can you balance the need for access to the right data while maintaining compliance with a changing regulatory and security landscape? Although there isn't one right answer, there are some best practices that can help turn the security officer into a business partner. Here are the top three:

1. **Work Together**

   Privacy, security, and project management offices must work together as a team. Many companies that proactively manage data privacy and security challenges embed privacy and security personnel within business units. Security by design should become a common strategy; this will help organizations build security and privacy provisions into projects from the outset.

2. **Assess Impact**

   Perform privacy and security impact assessments as part of a project's approval process. As a project moves forward, there should be continual checkpoints to ensure that compliance, security, and protection requirements are met. A project should not move forward with funding until it has been reviewed and the risk levels defined. Continuous assessments allow teams to identify and address issues in early stages of the project.

3. **Identify the Data**
   Identify the data that will be used for a new project. Understanding the sensitivity of data being used will make it easier for companies to meet the requirements of regulations such as the GDPR, and it will reduce the risk of a breach. Give business leaders and executives oversight of data based on the sensitivity and risks associated with the information. These executives should sign off on a project only once they agree that the risks of exposure are worth the benefits.

These best practices should be the foundation of an organization's security and governance policy as it prepares for the GDPR. This foundation will help protect the business from costly fines and will help prevent future security breaches.

Combining both organizational change with technical solutions can help organizations overcome the risks posed by removing data silos, giving employees access to more data and exploring new, data-centric business models. A well-planned strategy can enable an organization to innovate safely and securely.

The bottom line is that businesses should plan for more restrictions on access to their customers' personal data. The restrictions will develop based on a combination of new government regulations along with new customer demands.

Summary

What does it mean to manage the cycle of data in a well-governed and ethical manner? It is clear that you need to understand the nuances of managing your data with the right set of controls in place. Business leaders must understand the types of data insights that the business's data is producing. How are those insights getting operationalized? What risks do you face? Even if you are 100% legally clear, should you use certain insights?

With the proliferation of augmented intelligence, the risks will become more intense. Businesses will be able to predict the future and gain greater insights into what the data is telling them. Therefore, it is likely that there will be more opportunities to violate both the privacy of customer data and to unintentionally break governance rules. Corporate policies pertaining to data privacy and data permissions should be managed by a Chief Data Officer or Chief Compliance Officer. That officer is responsible for establishing corporate policies that meet statutory requirements and are consistent with customer expectations of transparency and fairness in the use of personal data.

The executive office (whether the Chief Data Office, Chief Compliance Office, or Chief Risk Office) cannot work in isolation. The planning and implementation of policies and controls should be done jointly with line managers who have responsibility for each business function. Ethical controls speak to the continuing human responsibility to govern the development and deployment of machine intelligence in order to ensure fair and safe operation. In the future, consumers along with regulators will be looking to businesses to act responsibly and transparently in gaining permission for the use of personal data.

Chapter 8

The Business Case for Augmented Intelligence

Introduction

Augmented intelligence is a powerful concept and a foundational technology that has the potential to transform data into a technique to predict customer behavior, provide a deep understanding of information, and plan for the future. Much of the excitement around artificial intelligence (AI) has been focused on using machine learning (ML) models to automate business processes. However, organizations that understand the power of creating collaboration between humans and machines can outpace the competition. In this chapter, we explore how businesses can capitalize on the power of augmented intelligence to gain an advantage, both in the short term and into the future as markets and competition change.

The Business Challenge

Organizations have never lacked data. In fact, most businesses have more data in various forms than they can manage and understand. The challenge has always been the complexity of extracting meaningful relationships or patterns about overall market dynamics and understanding how this relates to changing market conditions. How do you capture meaningful insights that aren't obvious? The problem goes beyond the ability to process data quickly—it is a problem of how to understand context and relationships that are meaningful, not simply anomalies.

The risks of inaction have never been higher. Emerging companies with little revenue are disrupting entire industries and markets overnight and causing established companies to scramble to create new strategies on the fly. Retailers have found that e-commerce has upended their business model, and to stay relevant they must engage with customers in new ways. Cab companies and vehicle manufacturers are being threatened by new ride sharing models. Manufacturing companies have found that innovative new automated processes and new supply chains have caused them to rethink their cost structures overnight.

It is not surprising that businesses must be able to understand hidden warnings about changes in market dynamics. The problem of being caught ill prepared for market transitions is not a new problem—it has plagued businesses for decades. Can artificial intelligence and machine learning models become tools to help businesses maintain their position in competitive markets? It is not simple to determine how organizations can gain the right level of insights to make a difference between success and failure. Simply automating processes and using weak augmentation is not the solution. To be successful, business leaders have to understand the data that defines their business—both structured and unstructured data—and then transform their business processes. To put this data to work requires that it is available in the right form to provide subject matter experts and leaders with the tools to accelerate change.

How does a business use the power of augmented intelligence to prepare for change? Data is only valuable in context with the business issue being addressed. It is not enough to have data about who your customers are, what they buy, and the problems they are having. This type of data will only let you understand what has happened in the past; it will not prepare you for the future. To be successful organizations need to take a holistic approach in order to gain insights from their data. What are the meaningful relationships or patterns from the data about your customers, partners, suppliers, and employees? What information can you find that indicates changes in customer buying patterns? Is there data about the availability of raw materials and how those prices are changing? Do you understand how customer preferences are different today from what they were five years ago or even two months ago? Are there changes in regulations that will impact your ability to satisfy customers? For example, if you are a financial services company, are you striking the right balance between giving customers easy access to their account information while also securing their data? Are governmental bodies establishing new regulations that will impact your business across the globe? There are countless examples of how businesses are being fined by governments for a lack of adherence to security and privacy requirements.

Do you truly understand how customer expectations are changing? A few years ago, it was common for businesses to charge customers for shipping. Now, customers are increasingly expecting that shipping will be included in the price of the product. Ironically, prices might be higher when shipping costs are built into the price but that may not deter customers from purchasing. It is critical that management understands the nuances of customer behavior and how it is changing as new business models emerge.

Taking Advantage of Disruption

Every era sees the advent of new technologies that disrupt the way we live, buy, and manage our lives. The steam engine transformed commerce in 1698; the telegraph invented in 1837 changed communications forever. Alexander Graham Bell's first US patent for the telephone in 1876 is the most transformative technology because it changed the pace of business as never experienced before. The invention of the automobile changed how individuals conducted their daily lives and how businesses transformed commerce. And, of course, the commercialization of the Internet in the early 1990s led to dramatic business changes. The Internet and then the advent of cloud computing and innovations in distributed computing has made the world of AI and machine learning commercially viable, as we discussed in Chapter 2. The bottom line is that what seems to be focused on a single purpose initially will often lead to dramatic changes in the way businesses must operate.

Disrupting Business Models

How can an organization take advantage of disruption to create new business models? First, it is important to recognize that dominating a market is no guarantee that this supremacy is sustainable. Today, it is possible for an emerging company to gain access to massive amounts of data that can be analyzed and understood in a way that can upend a market. One thing differentiates companies that can disrupt a market from those that succumb to the competition— data and how that data is analyzed. In fact, if you examine the companies that are upending markets and gaining credibility, they are businesses that have data at the core of their strategy.

However, it isn't enough to simply capture a lot of data. Rather, it is the ability to breakdown silos across data sources and integrate that data in significant ways. To be successful, these companies are extracting the patterns or relationships from the data in order to provide unique services. If you are able to understand what customers will need to buy based on their data, you will be in a better position to understand the nuances of their current and future requirements. Too often an online retailer will send an offer to a customer who has just purchased a product an opportunity to purchase the same product again. It would be more beneficial if the retailer were able to anticipate the next product that the customer might need based on that purchase. For example, customers who purchased a set of power tools may also need to purchase rechargeable batteries, a storage case, or other complementary tools and accessories. Making an attractive offer at the right time may increase the possibility of customers increasing their spending. Getting to the point of making the right offers to prospects at the right time requires being able to understand the relationships between products, the dynamics of the market, and customer buying patterns. Naturally, these patterns are not static. A product that is popular with customers one month may fade a few months later. The business that figures out innovative ways to put data to use in predicting customer trends and requirements will have a good chance to beat the competition.

Getting to the point where you can use data to anticipate the future and understand with certainty what customers need is complicated. To gain deep understanding requires that organizations are able to observe and capture data from external sources, ranging from social media data, demographic data, data about market trends, competitive data, research reports on the latest trends in a market, etc. The business needs to also leverage internal data—both structured data about customer trends and unstructured data about what customers are saying in their communications with the company. The ability to monetize data comes from the ability to discover what customers consider important and will be willing to pay for—even before the customer knows what they want.

Advantages of New Disruptive Models

One of the benefits of augmented intelligence is that it provides a machine learning approach that focuses on understanding the context of all types of data that are part of the core knowledge of the business. With augmented intelligence, it is possible to discover insights and patterns that would be difficult to understand without the support of advanced analytics. There will be situations, as we discussed in Chapter 1, in which your data is straightforward, and it is possible to easily automate in a consistent and predictable process. However, when you are dealing with complex and ever-changing business knowledge, it is likely that you will be using a corpus of data that can work in collaboration with subject matter experts. The value of this type of augmentation is critical to being able to disrupt a market. You cannot assume that an AI system will be able to easily discover the answers and solutions to complex problems. If, on the other hand, you can turn your massive amount of both structured and unstructured data into a well-engineered data platform, you can be prepared to plan for the future. This new augmented intelligence system will not necessarily provide immediate answers to complex problems. However, it will provide access and insights into patterns that experts can combine with their own understanding of their industry. The alternative approach requires that an expert manually discover patterns in complex data. The most experience experts will often know where to look and find the best sources of answers. However, often these experts are expensive to hire and in short supply.

The deeper meaning of information often remains hidden. Even if your industry experts have sufficient time, it is typical to miss key patterns and nuances hidden in data. In some cases, an expert may rely on techniques and knowledge related to how they have always thought about solving a problem. In competitive markets, you often need augmentation to be able to see the solution to a problem in a totally different light.

Managing Complex Data

It isn't enough to simply hope that the data scientists in your organization will have the knowledge and ability to make the most of your complex data. It is tempting to assume that these experts will take the right path in isolation from the business. When data scientists work in isolation from the business, they often make assumptions about what models should look like. In addition, they may not understand the nuances of the data they need to train to solve complex business problems. One of the key issues for business organizations is that management often does not understand the role of data scientists and therefore assumes that they understand the business. It is a difficult situation, since the cost of hiring a data scientist is very high. It is no wonder that upper management assumes that if you pay such a high salary, you are getting a professional who understands the business. This is often not the case.

Creating a Hybrid Team

The solution to taking advantage of the skills and knowledge of data scientists is to create a hybrid team. This team consists of a combination of different individuals that understand technology and the business. Who should be part of the team? The following provides you with some guidelines when constituting your team:

- **Business Analysts.** Analysts who understand the business are critical to the success of your team. These team members may be part of a business unit or provide guidance and understanding at the overall corporate level.
- **Business Strategists.** Strategists are in the best position to provide an understanding of where the company is headed. What are the new directions the company is headed in? What are the roadblocks in terms of the analysis that is needed to create a successful strategy? You want to make sure that the strategists are at a high enough level that they have a clear understanding of where the company is headed.
- **Data Analysts.** It is critical to have team members who understand the nature and characteristics of the business data across business units. What is the source of the data that the company relies on today? What data isn't available that would help in planning for the future of business processes?
- **Security and Governance Experts.** Team members who understand how to secure the data are critical to the success of your data initiatives. As you strategically move to augmented intelligence, you will have added responsibility to ensure that you are protecting sensitive data against inappropriate exposure.

Creating this team is instrumental in your success with augmented intelligence. However, simply bringing a team together is not enough. To be successful will require leadership. It is critical that the team understands their mission and goal and that there is upper management direction. Therefore, you need to select a team leader who can work with all of the constituents that are part of the process so that you have a successful outcome. Your outcome will be a data management environment that provides a way for experts to be able to leverage knowledge in a way that supports business goals.

The Four Stages of Data Maturity

All businesses deploy techniques to manage their data and use analysis of that data to make informed business decisions. However, organizations operate at different levels of sophistication and experience. Many organizations rely on traditional business intelligence reporting tools that provide insights into performance of various business units in terms of sales. Other businesses are moving to predictive analytics and are beginning to leverage machine learning models. As organizations gain more expertise, they are able to gain more insights into their businesses. Organizations that reach a higher level of maturity are able to take advantage of the knowledge and changing business processes to transform their organizations in light of new opportunities and challenges. A business does not get to the highest level of maturity overnight. Gaining this level of maturity requires building teams as well as gaining an understanding of the data you have and the data that you need.

Stage 1: Collecting Data from Multiple Sources That Has Been Vetted and Cleansed in Preparation for Reporting

During this stage, the data team begins to inventory the data that is available from a variety of systems, including corporate systems of record Enterprise Resource Planning (ERP), accounting systems, billing systems, customer management systems, etc. In addition, at this stage data analysts are beginning to bring in some unstructured data as a way to understand the nuances of customer engagement. The focus in Stage 1 is to make sure that data is accurate and integrated across silos. Often businesses will create a data warehouse or data mart to create a more manageable way to query and analyze current and past business performance. Therefore, the focus is on analyzing complex data in context with the state of the business. Creating this baseline is a critical step in having consistent and trusted knowledge about the business. Data cleansing and data integration techniques ensure that business leaders have the tools they need to accurately understand sales, operations, and finance. At this stage, predictions about the future of outcomes for the business will be based on currently available data. One of the problems is that this type of analysis is based on the assumption that the business environment will remain stable.

Stage 2: Focusing on Trend Analysis for Forecasting

This stage uses basic modeling capabilities to make business forecasts based on an analysis of historical trends. For example, a clothing buyer for a retail chain looks at past sales across the company's stores and forecasts next year's sales by store prior to placing a new order. The model is likely to account for various factors that differ across each of the stores such as climate, store location, and demographic characteristics of shoppers. The buyer may apply a What-If Analysis to adjust the sales forecast based on changes in selected variables. For example, what if next season has 5 or 10 additional heavy snowfall days? The forecast can be adjusted downward to account for less traffic in the store due to snowstorms. Although creating a forecast for the future based on past performance is a good place to start, these models were not designed to capture and account for change as it is happening. For example, the buyer in this example may end up with unsold merchandise after overlooking rapid changes in fashion trends among a certain demographic. The outcome from these systems tend to be based on the ability to codify current knowledge and report from those findings. In essence, the results of leveraging these systems are not predictive in nature. Rather, the results are based on a structured and well-defined set of problems.

Stage 3: Predictive Analytics

This stage is defined by the use of statistical or data-mining solutions that consist of algorithms and techniques that can be applied to both structured and unstructured data. Multiple sources of both structured and unstructured data types can be used individually or together to build comprehensive models. Some of the statistical techniques used in this phase include decision tree analysis, linear and logistic regression analysis, data mining, natural language processing, and time series analysis. A key factor in predictive analytics capabilities is having the ability to incorporate predictive models with business rules into the operational decision-making process. This makes the modeling process more actionable and helps businesses to improve outcomes.

The focus is on anticipating trends before they happen so that you can act to minimize risk for the business. Although predictive analytics has been used for many years by statisticians in certain industries, advances in software tools combined with increasing compute power has made this technology more accessible and more widely used by business users. Predictive analytics models are designed to analyze the relationships among different variables to make predictions about the likelihood that events will take place. For example, an insurance company may build a model that analyzes the components of fraudulent claims and use this model to flag claims that have a high probability of being fraudulent. Another common use case for predictive modeling is to help companies discover how to better provide customer service. For example, many wireless carriers are building predictive models designed to help call center agents answer questions more quickly. Based on the individual customer's profile, specific product recommendations can be made at the point of interaction between the agent and customer.

Stage 4: Prescriptive Analytics

Prescriptive analytics is intended to provide a technique that brings together information from many different sources to understand relationships in context. This is especially important in allowing humans to gain insights across massive amounts of unstructured data created in silos. Prescriptive and cognitive approaches take predictive analytics to the next level through techniques that bring in data from outside sources and apply sophisticated machine learning algorithms combined with advanced visualization and natural language processing to reach conclusions that can't be done in other ways. Companies want their models to look beyond their assumptions about the world so that they are better prepared to respond to changing market dynamics. If models are designed to continuously learn based on each new interaction, the accuracy will get better. For example, a satellite television provider has a predictive analytics model designed to help reduce churn. At the point of interaction with the customer, the customer service agents know which customers should be offered which type of deal to make sure they don't lose them as a customer. Previously, this satellite company used a model that was updated only every 6 months. The accuracy and sensitivity of the model to competitive changes in the marketplace was limited as a result. The company significantly improved its customer-retention rate by designing a new model that is more prescriptive. The model is designed to be self-learning by feeding each new interaction back into the model capturing changing market conditions. In addition, the model incorporates social analytics to understand the customer's interactions with and influence on others. These changes improved the model's capability to help drive accurate decision making regarding what the next best action should be to support the customer.

Models that are designed to adapt and change are beginning to be used by companies to predict when a machine is likely to fail so that corrective action can be taken before a catastrophic event occurs. For example, patterns identified in streams of machine data coming from sensors in a train can be used to build models that will anticipate equipment failure before it happens. By using adaptive learning, the model's accuracy can be continuously improved to provide a real-time warning of equipment failure in time for the company to take corrective action.

In addition to discovering patterns, companies need to be able to impart knowledge to employees with limited expertise. Defining best practices is a successful technique to help new employees create a dialog with a system. By codifying your best practices, knowledge is captured and refined over time. The promise of knowledge management was always difficult to achieve because it assumed that it would be possible to actively capture what experts knew. In contrast, using a cognitive approach, a system can ingest written information that can be vetted by experts. In addition, this same system can be trained as new information and new best practices emerge. This new dynamic knowledge source can become a competitive differentiator for a business. Imagine that employees with only a few weeks of experience can have immediate access to the right answers at the time of engagement with customers.

Building Business-Specific Solutions

There is a strong demand to create industry-specific augmented intelligence applications. The requirement for industry-focused applications stems from the fact that each industry has their own governance requirements, business challenges, and specific nuances. All of these solutions, whether we are looking at banking, transportation, or commerce, have common characteristics. The commonalities include:

- Large amounts of data in many different forms
- Industry-specific data (typically unstructured) that is constantly expanding
- The need to correlate a variety of data sources to determine context, patterns, and anomalies
- A requirement to find a way to match the data with deep expertise
- The need to analyze large amounts of data to support decision making, such as next best action
- The ability to have the systems learn and change as business conditions change

Augmented intelligence is changing the way people interact with computing systems, to help them find new ways of exploring and answering questions about their business. These systems will learn and interact to provide expert assistance to scientists, engineers, lawyers, and other professionals in a fraction of the time it now takes.

Making Augmented Intelligence a Reality

What makes augmented intelligence different is that these systems are built to change. The system continues to change based on the ingestion of more data and the ability to identify patterns and linkages between elements. The models are continually adjusting, rather than relying on previous data. Therefore, companies can look for associations and links between data elements that they might not even have known existed beforehand.

The results of creating these types of solutions can be profound. They enable a new level of engagement in which the business leader can have an intuitive interface between the system and the huge volume of data managed in the corpus. Even more important is that these systems are not static. As new data is added, the system learns and determines new ways of understanding situations. For example, new associations may suddenly appear that were not visible or present in the past. Perhaps there is an association between someone who buys books and takes a certain type of vacation. Perhaps there is a relationship between two drugs that can cause a never-before-seen interaction. There may be a new method of treating a serious condition based on a series of new research findings that were published only in the past month in an obscure journal.

The underlying value of augmented intelligence is that it has the potential to change the way individuals in organizations think about information. How do we ask systems about what the data we are seeing means? How can we interact with a system to provide insight when we don't know what direction to take or what question to ask?

It is becoming clear that we have only scratched the surface of the power of information managed in new ways to discover new ways to act and transform organizations.

How Augmented Intelligence Is Changing the Market

When industries are in transition with new competitive threats, it is impossible to simply build an application. Traditional applications are intended to automate processes and manage data. When a business is trying to transform a traditional industry such as travel or customer care, innovators need sophisticated technologies that allow leaders to discover new techniques and new knowledge. A travel company that can discover what customers want will have a differentiation. What if a travel company can know what the customer will buy even when the customer has no idea? What if a customer service representative can anticipate that the customer's problem is related to a partner's product within minutes rather than hours?

The new generation of solutions will look beyond codified practices and find the answers that are not obvious. Disrupters in every industry throughout the centuries have done precisely this: They have taken traditional approaches to solving problems and turned them upside down.

Summary

Augmented intelligence is emerging as a technical and cultural approach to analytics that has the potential to change the way humans interact with machines. Using machine learning and AI combined with the decision-making capabilities of humans is proving to be a transformational approach. It is important to remember that you cannot begin your journey by assuming that you will quickly transform every process within your company. In the next chapter, we discuss ways that you can approach getting started with augmented intelligence. The bottom line is that you have to focus on discrete business challenges and getting early wins in order to gain momentum. As you progress through the data-maturity stages, the value you are able to extract from your data will increase.

Chapter 9

Getting Started on Your Journey to Augmented Intelligence

Introduction

The potential to take advantage of the power of artificial intelligence (AI) and machine learning models is enormous. When organizations begin with data that is well understood, cleansed, and managed throughout the analytics process, the potential to transform business is significant. When armed with a wide array of machine learning libraries and open source technologies, subject matter experts can gain better insights into business opportunities. Professionals are now able to make well-informed decisions because they can apply their understanding of the business and customers to create a strategy that is based on data. As we discussed in Chapter 8, the business imperative is clear: Augmented intelligence is powered by a hybrid team of professionals who work in concert with emerging technologies to help power their organizations. In this chapter, we discuss how organizations can begin to create a successful plan to kick-start their journey to augmented intelligence.

Defining the Business Problem

The key to moving forward is to have a plan for getting started. If you start with too grand of a plan, you will get bogged down in a way that will lead to disappointment. Trying to completely reimagine your company on day one often leads to failure because teams are unable to see success quickly enough and you will soon lose momentum. On the other hand, if you pick too small a project, it will be difficult to show that the approach is worth the time and money. In this chapter, we discuss approaches that can help an organization get started with a roadmap and plan that helps create value to the business.

Before you begin to gather data and create a model, you first have to start with understanding your business objectives. Why is your organization considering augmented intelligence and machine learning models as part of your data strategy? Too often, a business that is struggling with competitive threats will look at emerging areas such as artificial intelligence as a lifeline. It is common to hear stories of threatened business leaders hoping that if they hire a team of data scientists, they will be able to reinvent their business and thrive. If only the solution were that simple. It is not possible to rely on hearsay and elusive promises to better understand and transform your business. Rather, you need to begin by understanding the current reality of your business's digital assets. Ironically, it is common for businesses to assume that because they have lots of data, they are ready to move to advanced analytics. Having a voluminous amount of data is important, but it is only the beginning. Here are the eight key categories of questions that you need to ask before you take action:

1. **Your own data.** How much data do you have about your customers, partners, and suppliers? Do you have enough data to understand the past as well as the present? Do you have a way of understanding what their future needs may be?
2. **Data reliability and truthfulness.** How accurate is the data that you have? Has it been evaluated and cleansed so that it reflects the true state of your business?
3. **Outside data sources.** Are there third-party data sources that will help you put the current reality of your business in context with what you understand and can analyze today?
4. **Distributed data.** Do you have disconnected silos of information across business units that are not shared today? Do you have a plan to bring those data sources together to gain a holistic understanding of the business?
5. **Security, privacy, and regulatory compliance.** Have you sufficiently secured and protected the sensitive data across the business so you will be free to apply advanced analytics without fear of breaking the rules?

6. **Business problem/decision.** Is the goal of the project to address a business problem or decision that is sufficiently important to the business to merit the dedication of resources to process improvement?
7. **Measurability of the improvement.** Can the business improvement be measured? Can you instrument the process so that you can collect financial metrics that will support a cost/benefit analysis for this project, as well as lay the groundwork for justifying the next project?
8. **Executive buy-in.** Do you have executive leadership overseeing your data strategy?

Maybe you can quickly address some of these questions but not others. To be successful in leveraging data for your business, you have to address all of the issues listed above. This is something that you cannot afford to compromise. For example, you may have a lot of data about your customers but do not know if the data is clean? Is there third-party data available to help enrich your customer data? Or have you done the work to prepare all your data in a responsible and accurate way? Different business units may be accessing third-party data sources. Who is responsible for assessing the accuracy of that data? Do you have a data catalog that defines the context of the data, such as its origins and its metadata? This will be fundamental in establishing a baseline for augmented intelligence.

Senior managers are impatient. They want to understand the relationship of data across lines of business. If you are a business leader, you want to understand the opportunities to sell existing products and services to existing customers. It is well understood that it is more cost effective to sell to a loyal customer than to find a new one. If there are loyal customers who buy products from one business unit, they may be ideal customers to buy from another business unit. Can you identify customers who are influential within their peer groups and who have the potential to become advocates for your company? You may have cooperation from some lines of business leaders but not others. Without executive leadership, it may be difficult to convince these lines of business leaders to collaborate to achieve important future business outcomes.

One of the reasons it is so important to have senior leadership buy-in is that you are trying to change the way the business thinks about the strategic role of data. A typical business unit head is tasked with building their individual business based on profitability and strategy. The last thing that business unit heads want to focus on is the overall goal of leveraging data across the entire organization. Business leaders are often evaluated on short-term goals rather than long-term strategy. Without a mandate from the top, it is too easy to simply ignore a project focused on gaining a strong approach to holistic data.

Clearly, there is a lot of preparation needed before a business can move from disconnected data sources to a consistent, trustworthy data environment that can be relied upon for critical decision making. Without careful planning and execution, you will be unable to move to augmented intelligence. In fact, you may want to consider beginning with advanced analytics as a starting point for your movement to augmented intelligence. Gaining a clear understanding of your data using packaged tools may be the best way to enable your team to make sense of your information at a fundamental level. For example, you may want to begin with some data visualization tools so that you can quickly understand what your data is telling you about your organization. How can you begin creating machine learning models that benefit your strategy without beginning with well-defined and understood data? The bottom line is that you cannot move forward in using your data for strategic advantage until you understand and manage your data.

Establish a Data Culture

It isn't enough to simply create a data platform. You need to establish a data culture across the company. Too often, business units are protective of their own information. This is not surprising, since a business area is judged on the quality of their customer engagement and how these relationships evolve into increasing revenue. Business leaders are often reluctant to share their data with a centralized data management organization. Their hesitancy to share information is part of the culture of the business. Business units may compete with each other for resources and do not want to give something away that could impact their position within the company.

Establishing a culture that fosters data collaboration begins at the top. Business leaders have to mandate data sharing and create a reward system. It is not as simple as saying that business units must share data. Leaders have to change the system that pits lines of business managers against each other. Many businesses have found that creating or promoting the position of Chief Data Officer (CDO) is critical to help the business shift to a data-centric culture. If empowered, the CDO can spearhead a culture of safely sharing data across divisions. The value of a data culture can impact all business units. Each area will be able to unleash new business opportunities as they gain insights from the shared data. One of the best ways to change the culture is to educate lines of business managers on the benefits of a new level of data analytics. Managers need to be able to appreciate the impact of augmented intelligence on the organization's ability to increase revenue across business units. This evolution to a data culture does not happen overnight. Once lines of business managers understand the value of the new focus on data, they must impart the same understanding to their teams.

Moving Forward with the Foundation

Once you have the fundamentals under control, you are in a good position to begin your initial implementation strategy. At this stage, it is important to assemble a team that represents a hybrid set of skills and knowledge. You will want to bring together team members from a variety of job functions, including technologists, leaders who are in contact with customers, business partners, executives, and experts in compliance and governance. Many organizations make the mistake of assuming that a data team will be able to do all the work necessary. However, this could not be further from the truth. Setting up the team with the right skills and the right knowledge will make the difference between success and failure. Therefore, you need subject matter experts. Depending on the scope of your business, you may need to have a team that represents all of the lines of business. You will need individuals who understand the current and future business processes. You will also need experts who understand your organization's underlying intellectual property and the elements that define your competitive differentiation. In addition, you will need business strategists who understand where the business is headed—both short and long term. These strategists need to be high enough in the organization that they can provide guidance to the team and have the credibility to be trusted.

Taking the First Steps

One of the common mistakes that businesses make is to try and create a massive data transition strategy across the entire company. Although it may be tempting to go big, it is often a mistake. If you do have a strategy to completely reimagine your data environment, to be successful, you need to break it up into achievable segments with measurable Key Performance Indicators (KPIs). There are countless stories of businesses spending millions of dollars on technology and employees to create a successful analytics or AI strategy, but failing to ever show meaningful results. Rather than making assumptions about the business's readiness for massive change, start with a project that will have business impact but is not so difficult that you risk failure. How do you pick their starting point? Here are some guidelines:

- Select a business unit that has strong management and has invested in its data platform. The business unit should already understand the potential impact of using data to transform their business area. There needs to be a senior manager who will champion the project and engage a cross-functional team to do the work.

- The business team that pilots your strategy should have well-understood and well-governed data. Where there are gaps, the organization must be able to determine what data is needed and acquire that data. This type of organization already understands the value of collaboration between subject matter experts and data experts.
- Finding the right project is imperative. There may be a project that is important to the organization, but it will be difficult to measure the business impact. Since this project will be the demonstration of the power of augmented intelligence, it must be able to demonstrate value so that other business units will be encouraged to follow the lead. In essence, you are building a reference that can be applied across the company.
- Salesmanship matters. Technology experts often assume that the value of emerging offerings is obvious. However, these professionals often lose sight of the fact that the underlying business value is misunderstood and mysterious to organizational leaders. Therefore, the teams responsible for these initial projects have to market and promote the value of their outcomes throughout the business. If you create a valuable outcome but no one knows what you have accomplished, it will not have the impact that you intend.

Selecting a Project that Can Be a Reference for Future Projects

A major airline invested in a team composed of data and analytical specialists who were in high demand across the company. Their mission was to take on projects that would drive process improvement and lead to better financial results. The manager of the group was frequently under pressure to take on projects that were the favorite ideas of senior managers. Unfortunately, there were more requests that swamped the capacity of the talented and high-performing team. How could the manager of the analytical team prioritize these requests?

One requirement for approval was that there must be sufficient data to gain significant results from analytic models. Some projects were eliminated from consideration because of a lack of relevant data, but there were still too many candidate projects that met this hurdle, given the resource constraints of the team. The availability of data, though a necessary condition, was hardly a sufficient condition for undertaking the project. This is because there must be an important business impact to justify the effort. The manager understood that investing resources in any single project came at a significant cost. Therefore, the outcome from a project needs to yield significant business benefits, and the results must be measurable. Two questions needed to be answered:

1. How much was at stake for the business if a process could be improved through the use of data and the implementation of data models?
2. Could the improvement be measured—that is, could benchmarks before the process change be compared to the results after the process change?

Let's take an example to see how these two points could be used to evaluate a candidate project. Consider a project designed to address fraudulent ticket discounting. The airline had sustained significant losses due to customers falsifying their current geographic location via the web and thereby obtaining fraudulent discounts. The company had existing anti-fraud models to detect dubious actions at the time of sale, but the new tactic of obtaining fraudulent discounts was not being detected. An important priority was that the airline wanted to avoid cancelling any tickets after they were purchased to avoid the risk of angering legitimate customers who were entitled to the discount. The airline needed to create a model that could identify fraudulent behavior while making sure that genuine customers were never disrupted. The airline's data team could develop new anti-fraud models that ingested transactional data as well as data gleamed from industry reports, historical information, and unstructured data found in security data feeds. The team would test and validate the models against transactions that they had identified as fraudulent over the last several months. In addition, the new models would have the potential to reduce the rate of false positives, which could reduce customer dissatisfaction when transactions failed because of suspicious behavior. There was clearly a significant potential saving to the company if the project proved successful. This endeavor would easily satisfy the first hurdle— the business criticality of the process improvement.

The second hurdle required that the results were measurable. Fortunately, there was data on the revenue lost due to tickets purchased using this fraudulent discounting technique. The new data models could be tested against previous transactions to understand how many fraudulent transactions would be caught. In addition, the rate of false positives was also known, and keeping this rate low was key in minimizing the chance of upsetting existing customers.

ATM transactions are in many ways similar to this airline example. When you go to an ATM, you expect to have a quick and easy transaction. Customers do not want to be challenged regarding the authenticity of their identity. Denying a legitimate customer access to their money is an easy way to lose customers and give them a reason to share their negative experiences with other

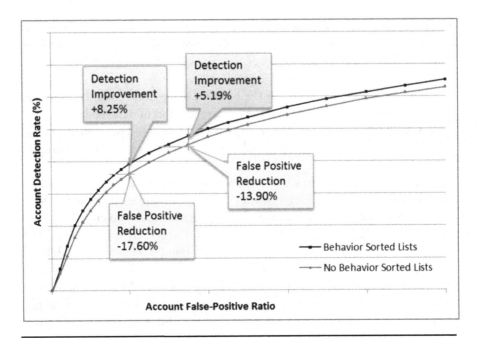

Figure 9-1   Demonstrating Model Improvement between Existing Fraud Model and Behavior-Based Model[1] (Reprinted with permission from FICO.)

current and potential customers. Figure 9-1 compares the performance of an ATM fraud-detection system between an existing model and a new technique for anti-fraud detection. The new model considered changes in the behavior of an individual from their established baseline of activity. This baseline can take into account the time of day the customer usually uses an ATM, the location of the ATM they usually use, and even factors like the time it takes to input a passcode. The new technique aimed to identify out-of-pattern activity while also reducing the rate of false positives.

Since the new approach to fraud looked promising, it was an easy decision to move ahead with the project. Fraud detection is a critical process to the company. The data existed to build the model. And the data about the process and previous transactions made it easy to test and validate the performance of the new model versus the existing model. There was sufficient accurate data to provide management with a valuable tool for identifying risk. These results would be used to not only justify the current investment but to also serve as a reference point for future projects on allied decisions—such as detecting other types of fraud.

Warning Signals

As you begin your journey toward augmented intelligence, your success may be predicated upon your ability to plan your strategy. You can't assume that everything will work as planned, or that you can scale your strategy without hard work. Here are some issues that can be warning signs that you need to consider before you can move forward toward success.

Are you ready to transfer knowledge?

You may start with a core team of both internal and external experts who have invested their time and effort into creating an outcome that provides business value to the company. This team will have to spend considerable time collaborating. What is the risk? To be successful with augmented intelligence, there needs to be a technique for transferring knowledge to other areas of the business. One of the best ways to accomplish this goal of exchanging best practices is to establish a center of excellence. This center will consist of experts from across the business who have gained experience from initial implementations. Therefore, the team needs to document both successes and failures that result from these initial efforts. As the center of excellence experiences success, they must begin to create repeatable best practices that other divisions can follow. At this point, the team can train new teams as they begin to implement their initial projects. These trainings should take the form of interactive workshops, where business units share their challenges, and together with the center of excellence, they can form a strategy. Without a center of excellence that focuses on knowledge transfer, you will be left with a standalone project and a strategy that cannot scale. The objective is to demonstrate success and then build on that success across the company.

Do you have enough data?

It is common to underestimate how much data you will need to gain significant insights into your analysis. You may have a lot of data regarding the products and services that your customers have purchased, but you don't have enough data about the overall market that you participate in. For example, there may be industry-specific technical journals in your field that include new research that can impact your strategy. Being able to access this unstructured data can be hugely helpful in understanding your market. You may need data about the changing demographics of your buyers. What will future customers need that they aren't buying today? What outside factors are going to impact your market? In addition, there are many third-party data providers. These third-party providers can provide you with valuable insights into customer demographics, competitors' customers, web-traffic patterns, weather trends, employment trends, and many more data sets. Many third-party data providers are focused on specific vertical markets, for example, finance, insurance, travel, entertainment, health and beauty, or retail. There are entire data marketplaces that are focused on connecting companies with data suppliers.

You may have a lot of unstructured data stored in various applications within your business that you never considered to be a data source. These data sources have been stored for years but have never been analyzed. This so-called "dark data" could include a wide variety of information, including customers' service call logs, email interactions with customers and partners, service tickets, employee resumes and applications, along with any other type of documented data. In addition, outside of your own company's digital assets, there is unstructured data on social media sites that includes information about your company's reputation and changing industry requirements. Turning this unstructured data into a corpus of usable information will help you gain clarity around your analytics. This dark data and data from social media may help provide insights about the performance of your company over time. For example, how has your interaction with customers changed over a decade? Are you having more data breaches than you had in the past? Are your customers happier than they were a decade ago? Have you been able to consistently improve your interactions with customers? Combining this data with your current understanding of the business will provide you with important insights that many competitors lack. In addition, new market entrants do not have the benefit of having years of data that can be mined.

Are you managing the process?

As you begin your pilot projects, you also need to focus on the overall management of the process. You need to make sure that as a hybrid team you are selecting the most important data sources. Don't be surprised if you have much more data than you would have expected. You will need to put some guardrails on the project—especially when you are doing a proof of concept or a pilot. If you make the scope of the project too big in order to leverage all of the data you have discovered, you may find that the project scope is too large. This doesn't mean that you need to get rid of this massive amount of data. Rather, you want to be able to select one part of that data and one bounded objective. Mapping all of your existing data resources to potential business opportunities will help you establish a roadmap for future projects that can result in significant gains.

Summary

Getting started is the first step toward creating a data culture within your organization. As we have discussed, it is important to establish pilots and teams that will be a model for your future steps. As we discussed in Chapter 3, you are dealing with a cycle of data, not a single step that leads you to positive outcomes and business success. Assume that creating a plan to continue to leverage new data and refine your models will require that this plan be constantly reviewed and revised. Part of your plan needs to assume and prepare for change.

Chapter 10

Predicting the Future of Augmented Intelligence

Introduction

We are still at an early stage in the evolution of machine learning, artificial intelligence (AI), and augmented intelligence. The key questions that organizations are asking are:

- Will AI take over the world and replace many of the jobs that people do?
- Will AI-driven systems be able to think for us?
- Will we be able to codify and leverage the knowledge in our organizations to make professionals able to do their jobs better?

Not surprisingly, the current business market for emerging technologies in the fields of AI and machine learning (ML) is quite confusing. The hype around the potential of AI and machine learning has risen to a level where some leaders assume that emerging technologies will be capable of automating every ordinary process a human can perform. Some experts have conjectured that deep learning systems will be designed to think like a human. Others experts are assuming that automated systems and robots will have the intelligence and ability to learn so that they will displace the vast majority of functions and jobs that people currently serve. In this chapter, we take a look into the future and provide our top predictions of what we can expect on the journey to augmented intelligence.

The Future of Governance and Compliance

Governance and compliance requirements will be built into models to satisfy governmental regulations and support the needs of management. Industry leaders will work with regulators to help codify rules and limitations on augmented intelligence systems. In addition, auditors will need to gain visibility into augmented intelligence systems to ensure that they are performing as expected. These governance capabilities will be designed to alert teams when something looks out of line with required compliance rules. However, automated functions will not prevail in every situation. When an alert is triggered, the system will provide guidance that experts can rely on to make better-informed decisions. At the same time, teams will also need to develop their own rules and follow their intuitions as well as their understanding in their area of expertise.

Regulation of any AI system is an emerging area because corporations and governments cannot assume consistent rules and policies due to constant changes in technology and business. In addition, human regulation relies on teams to anticipate problems and to respond when unanticipated problems occur. So new regulations need to be supported as they emerge (potentially via a software update) and added to company-specific standards. Business rules will be able to specify when an automated response to a potential violation should be triggered and when, alternatively, an alert should be sent to a human agent to make a decision on a remedial action. Furthermore, teams will always need to be aware of outcomes that seem suspicious. In many cases, an alert will not be generated, so it is important that the team examine the results of automated systems.

Professionals in all fields are asked to make decisions based on their knowledge and experience. An augmented system can provide both guidance in terms of providing research findings and best practices to the professional. There are times when the decision seems obvious. However, the obvious choice does not always serve as the right answer. Future requirements include having an augmented system look for anomalies in governance and privacy regulations, detect biases, and determine whether an AI-based decision contradicts a business best practice.

Emergence of Different Jobs

Will the hybrid collaboration of humans and machines result in fewer jobs for people? This is a subject upon which opinions differ widely. But what's clear is that the nature of work is already changing and will continue to change, reflecting the tradeoffs between what machines do best and what people do best. When machines automate more routine tasks, human experts can focus more on handling exceptions. For example, a call center bot handles frequently occurring questions rapidly and precisely. But the bot must be configured to hand off more complex and more risky questions to human agents. Likewise, an auditing bot can handle huge workloads, such as reviewing all transactions for signals of irregularities. But the bot hands off tasks to human auditors to investigate potentially fraudulent cases. When humans handle exceptions, they must get an informative alert with context from the machine, often with a recommendation on how to proceed. This is the future of augmented intelligence.

There will be many new jobs that do not exist today. With the advance of augmented intelligence into more domains, there will be a greater need for regulatory, governance, and ethical frameworks. Machines are not the source of such standards—that is the responsibility of humans. The many jobs that will be needed to manage augmented intelligence and handle machine-discovered exceptions have not existed before.

We cannot be sure at this point whether the jobs lost will exceed the jobs gained. Most likely, the largest category of all will be the jobs that are transformed via augmented intelligence, resulting in a far different mix of tasks than ever before. Those people who do not adapt to the changed nature of work will be the people at the greatest risk of loss of employment. But the greatest challenge for society, from a labor perspective, will be the massive training of those who are displaced by intelligent systems to fill the new jobs that augmented intelligence makes available.

Machines Will Learn to Train Humans

In the future, it will be possible to have a model observe employee actions and look for ways to improve them. However, this capability will not be a ubiquitous process in the workplace because of cultural issues. Observing people's actions and training them to perform with "better results" may make workers feel that they are devalued. On the other hand, workers may be more willing to have a system suggest process improvements that will help work become more successful. Imagine that you can use ML to train humans based on their data. There are some areas in which this approach could be non-threatening. For example, think about programs that help train an individual to become a better chess player. You play a chess game against the computer. The computer analyzes your moves and then explains how you could have made different moves in order to get better results. As you continue to play, the program provides interactive advice as you progress. This same process can be applied to any field in which employees' actions can be observed in order to improve the performance of tasks and in which they welcome ways to improve their performance. In essence, the system becomes an intelligent tutor. This will lead to new applications that will guide students based on the way they learn. The augmented intelligence system will be able to judge which areas the student needs additional help in and will guide the learning process. Therefore, the system will first have to diagnose the expertise of the learner and then present the most appropriate lessons at the right sequence. In an augmented system, humans will help to determine the areas of performance employees might be open to new training. Business leaders will work in collaboration with employees to identify these areas of potential improvement. Thus, the machine learning tools will be used in collaboration with people making decisions about where best to utilize those tools. This sort of collaboration between different teams of humans and the augmented AI system will result in the best outcome for the business.

New Techniques for Identifying Bias in Data

Emerging tools will support management's ability to identify biases in data that may not be apparent. Often business decision makers don't even realize that their decisions are biased. They assume that the data reflects a consistent, acceptable, and predictable model of reality. However, the data itself may be biased because it relies on previous and current data and best practices that are themselves biased against a certain group or organization.

A new generation of tools will be able to contribute to recognizing bias and recommend changes, such as including new data sources and the removal of data sources that are biased. Recommendations are straightforward in cases in which a model is inspectable and bias can be detected directly. But in cases where a model is not inspectable (as is typically the case), there must be support to evaluate the outcomes of automated decisions or recommendations made by the model—determining whether the actual decisions or recommendations reflect differential, adverse treatment against a protected class. These protected groups of people are defined in anti-discrimination laws such as the US Civil Rights Act of 1964, as well as local regulations, and include groups within a total population based on characteristics such as age, gender, race, or national origin. Often biases are shared by the organization, perhaps unwittingly, and so the recognition of bias is even more difficult. Businesses will need new ways to evaluate their standards and processes to ensure against hard-to-recognize biases.

Emerging Techniques for Understanding Unlabeled Data

Today, it is not easy to understand and interpret unlabeled data because there is no gold standard for building a model based on unlabeled data. In the future, there will be new techniques that will help data scientists to understand models created from unlabeled data. This innovation will accelerate the ability of organizations to make use of unstructured data to better understand the context of information for decision making. The upcoming systems to help understand models from unlabeled data will not appear soon. Current research is focused on making progress on this topic, but currently there have not been compelling results. Bringing research from the lab to the business world can be a slow process, so although we predict that results in this area will come about, it will not be in the next few years.

Emerging Techniques for Training Data

New techniques will emerge that make using data to create new models faster and more efficient. One of the most complex tasks for organizations is to have enough of the right data to accurately train a model. Emerging techniques will provide pretrained models that most closely reflect the type of model being developed. Once created, these pretrained models can be updated to reflect the nuances of the specific problem being addressed.

This scheme works as follows. Typically, a model is trained to handle a more general problem. That same model can then be modified to handle a more specialized version of the general problem. The benefit is that the special version will be able to be built with less new data. You only need to handle the differences that distinguish the specific case from the general situation that the original model was trained on. By providing the data based on the special case, the more general model can learn from its previous data plus data for the special case. For example, suppose a clothing retailer has a model for recommending outerwear to customers that purchase certain clothing. The general recommendation model can be customized to be more specific during a promotional period to only recommend shoes and boots. Of course, this approach only makes sense if you know what the general problem is, and if you know that your problem is really a special case of the general problem. If the model were inspectable, this knowledge would be relatively straightforward to obtain, but in the case of models from black box algorithms, you have to do a lot more guessing about the shape of the general model and whether your problem really is a special case of the general model. However, people working with the general model are likely to come to know what it does well, and so the human-in-the-loop can provide the assessment needed to judge what the general model really does.

Reinforcement Learning Will Gain Huge Momentum

Although much of the focus in recent years has been around deep learning, deep reinforcement learning (RL) is emerging as a powerful technique that combines neural network modeling with reinforcement learning. The power of reinforcement learning comes from its ability to have a system learn to take next actions based on trial and error. It is a powerful technique for when you need to determine a series of actions required to achieve a goal or reward. This technique has been successfully applied to games wherein the player takes an action and then must respond to the next action taken by another player. Two examples of where RL is commonly used in a business context are marketing and customer services. In marketing, reinforcement learning can help determine the next step to take as a customer or prospect progresses down the path toward a sale. For customer service, the system helps to guide a service agent on the next best action to take when interacting with a customer. Deep learning provides the ability to analyze and learn from layers of hidden patterns. Combining reinforcement learning with neural networks could provide a much richer platform that understands context and learns from actions in order to transform business processes based on experience.

The use of reinforcement learning to make business decisions has left the research lab and is in use in business. For example, this model can be applied to the loan industry, wherein an algorithm can help determine the best series of steps to follow to successfully encourage a person to pay back a debt.

Using deep neural networks to understand the policies (rules) chosen in RL would have huge implications for business, since it could help management understand why the RL algorithm created this specific rule. However, this area of research is just barely started. So if it succeeds, it will be very useful.

New Algorithms Will Improve Accuracy

The emergence of new algorithms will improve the accuracy of machine learning models. Currently, there are more than 40 key machine learning algorithms widely used for a variety of applications in science and business. Because organizations want to be able to integrate vision, speech, sound, and smell into their models, there will be new algorithms developed, or combinations of existing ones used, that will understand the nuances of these data types. One example, OpenAI's new algorithm, called GPT-2, is designed for language modeling and makes use of a program's ability to predict the next word in a given sentence. This capability increases the ability to generate sentences and stories. Give it a fake headline, and it'll write the rest of the article, complete with fake quotations and statistics. Feed it the first line of a short story, and it'll tell you what happens to your character next. It can even write fan fiction, given the right prompt. Although this very recently developed algorithm does not integrate vision, speech, and so on, it indicates that new techniques developed over the next 10 years might have rather surprising capabilities.

Distributed Data Models Will Protect Data

One of the issues that organizations have to grapple with is the need to move sensitive data outside of their organization in order to execute machine learning models. Techniques that enable a business to move the model to the data rather than moving the data will provide more secure methods of protecting data security during analytic processing. An emerging approach is data virtualization. Data virtualization allows organizations to manage data access and manipulate and query data without having to move the data into a single repository or warehouse. In essence, data virtualization is a peer-to-peer architecture whereby queries are broken down and sent closer to the data sets. After all the subqueries are processed, results are combined along the way, thus eliminating the application entry point/service node as the bottleneck. Data virtualization allows organizations to analyze data where it resides rather than requiring that the data be moved to a different location.

Explainability Will Become a Requirement

Providing guidance to experts through an augmented intelligence system requires that developers and business management understand how the results were arrived at, and the level of confidence the model has in the results. There is a huge risk if an expert simply accepts a conclusion or answer blindly. Machines are only as good as the developers of the model. In the future, therefore, models will have greater transparency—or inspectability—so that there is an explanation for how the model reached its conclusion. This is necessary for dealing with legal challenges to decisions based on a model—where a consumer would seek to understand why he/she received a particular score that impacted credit or hiring.

Linking Business Process to Machine Learning Models

The next stage in model creation is to have a way to link related business process machine learning models together. For example, an insurance business that sells both mortgages and car loans may be able to link those data models so that it is easier to make decisions based on how data about an individual or organization is related. If one individual has defaulted on a mortgage and is asking for a car loan, linking these data models together will help decision makers evaluate risk. The revelations from linking models will help developers evolve the models so that they are more accurate. An important concept to consider is that many businesses have over-relied on single sources of data, or data that is aggregated from similar sources, to link data.

For example, a business that extends credit to customers, such as a furniture store, an auto dealership, landlords, or a financial institution, often relies on an individual's credit score. A person's credit score, which was intended to predict the likelihood of a borrower to repay a loan, has now become a measure of an employee's level of responsibility. Checking a potential employee's credit score is now a common practice among many businesses. This expanded use of a credit score has penalized perfectly good customers or employees, and it might be seen as an unfair business decision. Regulatory bodies have been slow to respond to the broadening use of data, such as credit scores. In general, the extension of the intended use of a data aggregate to another domain is hard to control—for example, the use of a drug for a non-intended purpose—and is a problem for the model developer who did not authorize the use but could be held responsible for the consequences.

Summary

We are at an exciting inflection point in the movement toward artificial intelligence and machine learning. Augmented intelligence has the potential to put these technologies to work in a way that opens up huge opportunities to create a hybrid collaboration between humans and machines for solving real-world challenges. There will be a variety of new techniques that will help augmentation become more reliable and predictable. Although some of these predictions are around the corner, other techniques will take time and attention before they become mainstream.

References

Chapter 1

1. Scism, L. (2017, May 23). "Insurance: Where Humans Still Rule Over Machines." *The Wall Street Journal*. Retrieved from https://www.wsj.com/articles/insurance-a-place-where-humans-not-machines-rule-1495549740

2. Anderson, M. (2017, May 11). "Twenty Years on from Deep Blue vs Kasparov: How a Chess Match Started the Big Data Revolution." Retrieved August 28, 2019, from http://theconversation.com/twenty-years-on-from-deep-blue-vs-kasparov-how-a-chess-match-started-the-big-data-revolution-76882

3. Cassidy, M. (2017, December 6). "Centaur Chess Shows Power of Teaming Human and Machine." *HuffPost*. Retrieved from https://www.huffpost.com/entry/centaur-chess-shows-power_b_6383606

4. Mercatus Center. (2017, May 10). "Garry Kasparov on AI, Chess, and the Future of Creativity" (Ep. 22). Retrieved August 26, 2019, from https://medium.com/conversations-with-tyler/garry-kasparov-tyler-cowen-chess-iq-ai-putin-3bf28baf4dba

5. McCarthy, J., Minsky, M. L., Rochester, N., and Shannon, C. E. (1955, August 31). "A Proposal for the Dartmouth Summer Research Project on Artificial Intelligence." (Reproduced in *AI Magazine*, vol. 27, no. 4 [2006]; https://doi.org/10.1609/aimag.v27i4.1904.)

6. Simon, H. A. (1965). *The Shape of Automation for Men and Management*, p. 96. Harper & Row. (Cited by Raymond Kurzweil in "What Is Artificial Intelligence Anyway?" *American Scientist*, vol. 73, no. 3 [May–June 1985], pp. 258–264.)

7. Minsky, M. L. (1967). *Computation: Finite and Infinite Machines*, p. 2. Upper Saddle River (NJ): Prentice-Hall, Inc. (Cited by Aggarwal, A. [2018]. "The Birth of AI and the First AI Hype Cycle." KDNuggets.) Retrieved from https://www.kdnuggets.com/2018/02/birth-ai-first-hype-cycle.html

8. Licklider, J. C. R. (1960, March). "Man-Computer Symbiosis." *IRE Transactions on Human Factors in Electronics*, vol. HFE-1, no. 1, pp. 4–11. Retrieved from https://ieeexplore.ieee.org/document/4503259

9. Engelbart, D. C. (1962, October). "Augmenting Human Intellect: A Conceptual Framework." (Prepared for Director of Office of Information Sciences, Air Force Office of Scientific Research.) Retrieved from https://www.dougengelbart.org/pubs/papers/scanned/Doug_Engelbart-AugmentingHumanIntellect.pdf

10. Tversky, A. and Kahneman, D. (1973). "Availability: A Heuristic for Judging Frequency and Probability." *Cognitive Psychology*, vol. 5, pp. 207–232.

11. Tversky, A. and Kahneman, D. (1974). "Judgment under Uncertainty: Heuristics and Biases." *Science (New Series)*, vol. 185, pp. 1124–1131.

12. Kahneman , D., Slovic, P., and Tversky, A. (1982). *Judgment under Uncertainty: Heuristics and Biases*. New York (NY): Cambridge University Press.

13. Kahneman, D. and Tversky, A. (1979). "Prospect Theory: An Analysis of Decision under Risk." *Econometrica*, vol. 47, no. 2, pp. 263–292; https://doi.org/10.2307/1914185

14. Bostrum, N. (2014). *Superintelligence: Paths, Dangers, and Strategies*. Oxford University Press.

15. "King with the Power to Turn Whatever He Touches to Gold." (2019, August 26). Retrieved August 26, 2019, from https://en.wikipedia.org/wiki/Midas

Chapter 3

1. Colarusso, D. (2015, July 29). "Bureaucrats and Mathemagicians: Data Science and the Public Defenders." Retrieved August 28, 2019, from https://www.lawtechnologytoday.org/2015/07/data-science-public-defenders/

2. Meier, D. (2013). The Identification of Individuals Potentially Affected by the Alleged Conduct of Chemist Annie Dookhan at The Hinton Drug Laboratory—Final Report to Governor Deval Patrick. Retrieved from https://archives.lib.state.ma.us/bitstream/handle/2452/205819/ocn856540987.pdf?sequence=3&isAllowed=y

3. Schuppe, J. (2017, April 18). "Epic Drug Lab Scandal Results in More Than 20,000 Convictions Dropped." Retrieved August 27, 2019, from https://www.nbcnews.com/news/us-news/epic-drug-lab-scandal-results-more-20-000-convictions-dropped-n747891

4. "Zillow Prize: Zillow's Home Value Prediction (Zestimate)—Can You Improve the Algorithm That Changed the World of Real Estate?" (2017). Retrieved August 27, 2019, from https://www.kaggle.com/c/zillow-prize-1

5. Zillow, Inc. (2018, March 1). "Zillow Awards First Round Prizes in Zestimate 0 Competition 100 Teams Advance to the Second Round of the Zillow Prize Competition to Improve the Zestimate's Accuracy." Retrieved August 27, 2019, from http://zillow.mediaroom.com/2018-03-01-Zillow-Awards-First-Round-Prizes-in-Zestimate-Competition

6. "Zillow Launches $1 Million Zestimate Competition for Data Scientists." (2017, May 24). Retrieved August 27, 2019, from https://www.prnewswire.com/news-releases/zillow-launches-1-million-zestimate-competition-for-data-scientists-300462943.html

7. "Exploratory Analysis—Zillow." (2017). Retrieved August 27, 2019, from https://www.kaggle.com/philippsp/exploratory-analysis-zillow

Chapter 4

1. Bean, R. (2018, March 15). "How American Express Excels As A Data-Driven Culture." Retrieved August 29, 2019, from https://www.forbes.com/sites/ciocentral/2018/03/15/how-american-express-excels-as-a-data-driven-culture/

Chapter 5

1. Kraljic, P. (1983). "Purchasing Must Become Supply Management." *Harvard Business Review*, vol. 61, no. 5, pp. 109–117. Retrieved from https://hbr.org/1983/09/purchasing-must-become-supply-management%20DOI
2. Safdar, K. (2016, November 27). "As Gap Struggles, Its Analytical CEO Prizes Data Over Design." *The Wall Street Journal*. Retrieved from https://www.wsj.com/articles/as-gap-struggles-its-analytical-ceo-prizes-data-over-design-1480282911
3. Israeli, A. and Avery, J. "Predicting Consumer Tastes with Big Data at Gap." Harvard Business School Case 517-115, May 2017. (Revised March 2018.)
4. Safdar, K. (2019, February 28). "Gap to Split Into Two Public Companies." *The Wall Street Journal*. Retrieved from https://www.wsj.com/articles/gap-to-split-into-two-publicly-traded-companies-11551389463
5. Steinmetz, K. (2018, May 3). "Stitch Fix Has One of Silicon Valley's Few Female CEOs. But the Company Stands Out for More Than That." *Time*. Retrieved from https://time.com/5264160/stitch-fix-has-one-of-silicon-valleys-few-female-ceos/

Chapter 7

1. Dwoskin, E. (2019, January 25). "YouTube Is Changing Its Algorithms to Stop Recommending Conspiracies." *The Washington Post*. Retrieved from https://www.washingtonpost.com/technology/2019/01/25/youtube-is-changing-its-algorithms-stop-recommending-conspiracies/
2. Vedantam, S. (Host). (2016, May 17). "Hidden Brain" [Audio Podcast]. Retrieved from https://www.npr.org/2016/05/17/478266839/this-is-your-brain-on-uber
3. Duhigg, C. (2012, February 25). "How Companies Learn Your Secrets." *The New York Times*. Retrieved from https://www.nytimes.com/2012/02/19/magazine/shopping-habits.html?pagewanted=1&_r=1&hp
4. "Facebook–Cambridge Analytica Data Scandal." (2019). Retrieved August 27, 2019, from https://en.wikipedia.org/wiki/Facebook%E2%80%93Cambridge_Analytica_data_scandal
5. Art. 13 GDPR—"Information to be Provided Where Personal Data Are Collected from the Data Subject—General Data Protection Regulation (GDPR)." (2016, August 30). Retrieved August 29, 2019, from https://gdpr-info.eu/art-13-gdpr/

6. "Art. 14 GDPR—Information to be Provided Where Personal Data Have Not Been Obtained from the Data Subject—General Data Protection Regulation (GDPR)." (2016, October 6). Retrieved August 29, 2019, from https://gdpr-info.eu/art-14-gdpr/

7. "Art. 15 GDPR—Right of Access by the Data Subject—General Data Protection Regulation (GDPR)." (2018, March 28). Retrieved August 29, 2019, from https://gdpr-info.eu/art-15-gdpr/

8. "Art. 16 GDPR—Right to Rectification—General Data Protection Regulation (GDPR)." (2018, March 28). Retrieved August 29, 2019, from https://gdpr-info.eu/art-16-gdpr/

9. "Art. 17 GDPR—Right to Erasure ('Right to be Forgotten')—General Data Protection Regulation (GDPR)." (2017, June 12). Retrieved August 29, 2019, from https://gdpr-info.eu/art-17-gdpr/

10. "Art. 18 GDPR—Right to Restriction of Processing—General Data Protection Regulation (GDPR)." (2016, August 30). Retrieved August 29, 2019, from https://gdpr-info.eu/art-18-gdpr/

11. "Art. 20 GDPR—Right to Data Portability—General Data Protection Regulation (GDPR)." (2018, March 28). Retrieved August 29, 2019, from https://gdpr-info.eu/art-20-gdpr/

12. "Art. 21 GDPR—Right to Object—General Data Protection Regulation (GDPR)." (2018, March 28). Retrieved August 29, 2019, from https://gdpr-info.eu/art-21-gdpr/

13. "Art. 22 GDPR—Automated Individual Decision-Making, Including Profiling—General Data Protection Regulation (GDPR)." (2018, July 26). Retrieved August 29, 2019, from https://gdpr-info.eu/art-22-gdpr/

Chapter 9

1. Zoldi, S. (2014, July 21). "Research: New Analytics That Boost Fraud Detection." Retrieved September 12, 2019, from https://www.fico.com/blogs/research-new-analytics-boost-fraud-detection

Index

Printed in the United States
by Baker & Taylor Publisher Services